THE GREAT GLEN

MONADHLIATH

AND MORAY

THE GREAT GLEN
MONADHLIATH
AND MORAY

A personal survey of the Great Glen,
Monadhliath and Moray
for mountainbikers and walkers

by

Peter D. Koch-Osborne

CICERONE PRESS
MILNTHORPE CUMBRIA

© P. D. Koch - Osborne 1997
ISBN 1 85284 236 9

British Library Cataloguing-in-Publication Data.
A catalogue record of this book is
available from the British Library.

Across the moorland, past the mountains
O'er the rivers, beside the new streams
Something tells me that I'm going home
"Going Home", written by :-
Calum MacDonald + Rory MacDonald.
©Chrysalis Music Ltd.
Used by permission. All Rights Reserved.

Cover pictures :- Dulnain to Lynwilg
Glen Roy

Index

Introduction

Access to the tracks on the following pages can rarely be regarded as an absolute right by the cyclist or walker. Almost all land is private and it is often only the good nature of the owners that allows us to travel unhindered over his land. In Scottish law the term trespass implies nuisance or damage. In practice sensible conduct removes any possibility of nuisance. Respect the grouse season (12 Aug to 10 Dec) and deer stalking (1 Jul to 20 Oct - stags and 21 Oct to 15 Feb - hinds). Your author has not once met with animosity in meeting 'keepers. Your good conduct will ensure continued access. Cyclists - stay on the trail and slow down!!

Conservation of the wild areas of Scotland is of paramount importance. Much has been written elsewhere but users of this guide must appreciate that the very ground over which you walk or cycle will be damaged if care is not taken. Please don't use a bike on soft peat paths and tread carefully on other than a stony track. Many of the tracks are in themselves an eyesore and any "development" can cause irreparable damage. Make sure, as walkers and cyclists, we encourage the conservation of our wilderness areas without the pressure of our activities causing further damage. In publishing this book a great deal of trust is placed upon you, the reader, to respect the needs of the region. If all you need is exercise - go to a sports centre! but if you appreciate the unique qualities of the wild places they are yours to enjoy..... carefully! Careless conduct not only damages what we seek to enjoy but, equally seriously, gives landowners good reason to restrict access.

The Maps on the following pages give sufficient detail for exploration of the glens but the Ordnance Survey Landranger maps of the region should also be used if the full geographical context of the area is to be fully appreciated. These maps and the knowledge of their proper use are essential if a long tour or cross country route is to be undertaken.

The mountain bike, or ATB - all terrain bike, has in the author's opinion been badly named. It does not belong on the high tops but is ideal in the glens covering at least twice the distance of the average walker, quietly, whilst still allowing a full appreciation of the surroundings and providing further exploration into the wilderness especially on short winter days. The bike must be a well maintained machine complete with a few essential spares as a broken bike miles from anywhere can be serious. Spare gear is best carried in strong panniers on good carriers. Poor quality bikes and accessories simply will not last. Front panniers help distribute weight and prevent "wheelies". Mud-guards are essential. Heavy rucksacks are tiring and put more weight onto one's already battered posterior! The brightly coloured "high profile" image of mountainbiking is unsuited to the remote glens. These wild areas are sacred and need treating as such.

Clothing for the mountainbiker is an important consideration, traditional road cycling gear is un-suitable. High ankle trainers are best for summer, and light weight walking boots for winter cycling. A zipped fleece jacket with waterproof top and overtrousers with spare thin sweatshirts etc should be included for easily adjusting temperature. The wearing of a helmet is a personal choice, it depends how you ride, where you ride and the value you place on your head! In any event a thin balaclava will be required under a helmet in winter or a thick one in place of a helmet. Good waterproof gloves are essential. Fingers and ears get painfully cold on a long descent at −5°C. Protection against exposure should be as for mountain walking. Many of the glens are as high as English hilltops. The road cyclist's shorts or longs will keep legs warm in summer only. In winter walker's breeches and overtrousers are more suitable.

Clothing for the walker has had much written about it elsewhere. Obviously full waterproofs, spare warm clothing, spare food etc. should be included. In winter conditions the longer through routes should never be attempted alone or by the inexperienced.

Mountainbikers and walkers alike should never be without a good map, this book (!), a whistle (and knowledge of its proper use), compass, emergency rations, and in winter a sleeping bag and cooker may be included even if an overnight stop is not planned. Word of your planned route should be left together with your estimated time of arrival. The bothies must be left tidy with firewood for the next visitor. Don't be too proud to remove someone else's litter. Join the Mountain Bothies Association to help support the maintenance of these simple shelters. It should not be necessary to repeat the Country Code and the Mountain Bike Code, the true lover of the wild places needs peace and space - not rules and regulations.

River crossings are a major consideration when planning long or "through" routes virtually anywhere in Scotland. It must be remembered that snowmelt from the high mountains can turn what is a fordable stream in early morning into a raging torrent by mid afternoon. Walkers should hold on to each other, in three's, forming a triangle if possible. Rivers can be easier to cross with a bike, as the bike can be moved, brakes applied, leant on, then the feet can be re-positioned and so on. The procedure is to remove boots and socks, replace boots, make sure you can't drop anything and cross - ouch! Drain boots well, dry your feet and hopefully your still dry socks will help to warm your feet up. Snowmelt is so cold it hurts. Choose a wide shallow point to cross and above all don't take risks.

Ascents on a bike should be tackled steadily in a very low gear and sitting down wherever possible. While front panniers prevent "wheelies" sitting down helps the rear wheel grip. Standing on the pedals causes wheel slip, erosion, and is tiring. Pushing a laden mountainbike is no fun and usually the result of tackling the lower half of a climb standing up, in the wrong gear or too fast.

Descents on a bike can be exhilarating but a fast descent is hard on the bike, the rider, and erodes the track if wheels are locked. It is also ill-mannered towards others who may be just around the next bend.

Last but not least other users of the tracks need treating with respect - it may be the owner! Bad conduct can only lead to restricted access, spoiling it for us all.

The Maps 1

The maps are drawn to depict the most important features to the explorer of the glens. North is always at the top of each map and all maps, apart from the detail sketches, are to the same scale :- 1km or 0·6 miles being shown on each map. An attempt has been made to present the maps in a pictorially interesting way. A brief explanation of the various features is set out below :-

Tracks :- One of the prime objects of this book is to grade the tracks according to "roughness". This information is essential to the mountainbiker and useful to the walker. With due respect to the Ordnance Survey one "other road, drive or track" can take twice as long to cycle along as another yet both may be depicted in the same way. The author's attempt at grading is set out below :-

metalled road, not too many fortunately, public roads are generally included only to locate the start of a route.

good track, hardly rutted, nearly as fast as a road to cycle on but can be boring to walk far on.   Most are forest tracks.

the usual rutted "Landrover" track, rough but all easily rideable on a mountainbike, not too tedious to walk on.

rough, very rutted track nearly all rideable, can be very rough even for walking. Either very stony or overgrown or boggy.

walker's path, usually over 50% is rideable and included especially as a part of a through route. Details given on each map.

<u>Relief</u> is depicted in two ways. The heavy black lines are now a commonly used method of depicting main mountain summits, ridges and spurs thus:-

Contour lines are also used, at 50m intervals up to about 600m. This adds "shape" to the glens as mapped and gives the reader an idea of how much climbing is involved. Reference to the gradient profiles at the start of each section compares the various routes:-

500m   550m   600m

<u>Crags</u> in the high mountains are shown thus:-
....with major areas of scree shown dotted

<u>Rivers</u> generally "uncrossable" are shown as two lines whilst streams, generally "crossable" are shown using a single line. Note:- great care is needed crossing even the larger streams. Falling in can cause embarrassment at best, exposure or drowning at worst. Please don't take risks - besides you'd get this book wet !!

loch or lochan

<u>Buildings</u> and significant ruins are shown as a:- ■

<u>Bridges</u> are rather obviously shown thus:- ✕
There are so many trees I wish there were an easier way of drawing them - but there isn't! I'm fed up with drawing trees!!

etc etc.....

11

The Great Glen, Monadhliath and Moray - West

Map of The Great Glen, Monadhliath and Moray showing land over 600m or 2000ft. A more detailed map of each area precedes each section :- 'The Great Glen', 'South West Monadhliath', 'North East Monadhliath' and 'Moray'. Feasible through or 'Link' routes are given in the final section of this book.

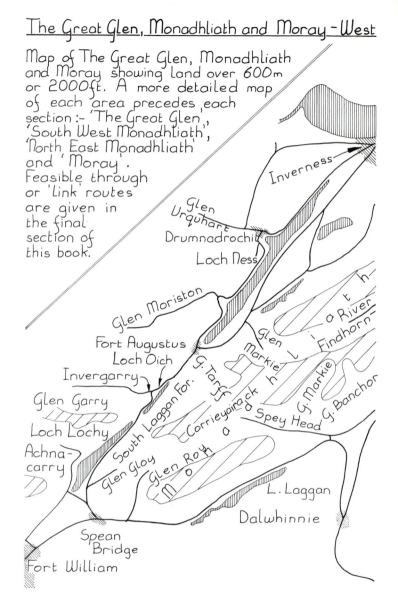

The Great Glen, Monadhliath and Moray-East

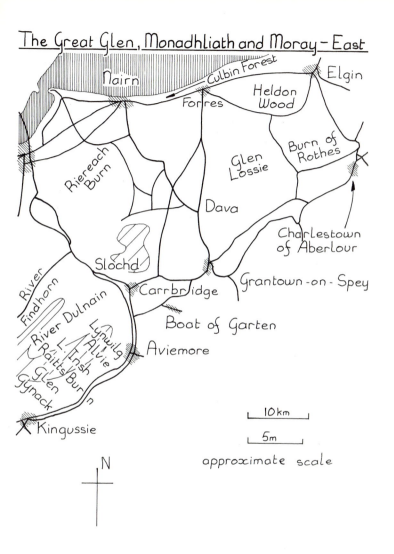

Nairn
Culbin Forest
Elgin
Forres
Heldon Wood
Burn of Rothes
Riereach Burn
Glen Lossie
Dava
Charlestown of Aberlour
Slochd
River Findhorn
River Dulnain
Lynwilg
Alvie
L. Insh
Raitts Burn
Glen Gynack
Carrbridge
Grantown-on-Spey
Boat of Garten
Aviemore
Kingussie

10 km
5 m
approximate scale

N

The Great Glen

The Great Glen

Access:- My usual section on access is extended to explain the nature of the Great Glen Cycle Route. Access is, in any event, obvious with the main centre of Fort William at the usual start, and Inverness some 15miles from the finish at Drumnadrochit. It must be stressed that the GGCR is NOT an alternative to the A82 for the road cyclist. The GGCR is a mountainbike route, also ideal for the long distance walker. For the road cyclist there is no safe route up the Great Glen and plans should be made accordingly. Reference to the gradient profiles and close study of the map pages depicting the purpose-built steep path sections confirm the above. Please don't use the A82!! Your author is convinced the GGCR puts more cyclists on the A82 than the intended opposite as disillusioned cyclists simply give up the struggle! The run into Inverness may be:-1/ by minor roads from Fort Augustus south east of Loch Ness (via an enormous hill!); 2/ by the recommended route from Drumnadrochit via Abriachan (via another big hill); or 3/ by Glen Urquhart, Cannich, Strathglass(minor rd.), Beauly, north of the Beauly Firth, then the Kessock Bridge cycleway into Inverness. This latter option is the longest and, in your author's opinion, best.

Accommodation:- Fort William and Inverness boast all types of accommodation, most of which is fully booked in summer. Fort Augustus and Drumnadrochit are the only other centres. Between the above centres hotels and B+Bs are spread thinly. Your author's recommendation is to use the S.Y.H.A. hostels at Glen Nevis (for Ft. Bill); Loch Lochy(also for S.

16

Laggan Forest); Loch Ness and Cannich.
Geographical Features :- The Great Glen, or more correctly Glen Mor is formed by a geological fault line which extends from north of Jura to Tarbat Ness providing a natural communications link right across Scotland. However these communications are limited by the difficulties encountered along the steep shores of Loch Ness - the railway was never completed - nor yet the cycle route! The Caledonian Canal uses the lochs and had no such problems when built. Even General Wade went south (over the Corrieyairack) and east to Stratherrick from Fort Augustus.

Mountains:- Views to the high mountains are finest around Lochaber, the glen is more open and the mountains higher. The steep sides of central Glen Mor and Loch Ness conceal the best of the Monadhliath mountains. Ben Tee, north of Loch Lochy is prominent from Loch Oich to Loch Ness.

Rivers:- The Great Glen is drained to the south west by the River Lochy and to the north east by the Rivers Oich and Ness. The Rivers Spean and Arkaig swell the River Lochy whilst the Garry, Tarff and Moriston add their contribution to the Oich and Ness.

Forests:- South Laggan Forest flanks Loch Lochy whilst Inchnacardoch Forest overlooks Fort Augustus. Portclair and Creag nan Eun Forests lie either side of Invermoriston. There is little natural woodland other than along the south east shore of Loch Oich.

Lochs:- Loch Ness reigns supreme - size alone confirms that! Loch Lochy is spoilt by the road so close to its shore. For scenic beauty your author's vote goes to Loch Oich.

The Great Glen Routes 1

Fort William to Achnacarry

Fort William (centre) — Neptune's Staircase — Caledonian —50m— Canal — Gairlochy — Achnacarry (A)

0 1 2 3 4 5 6 7 8 9 0m 10 11 12 13 14 15 16km 17

Achnacarry to Invergarry

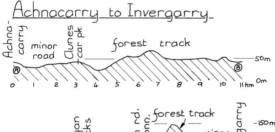

Achnacarry (A) — minor road — Clunes car pk. — forest track — (B) — 50m — 0m

0 1 2 3 4 5 6 7 8 9 10 11km

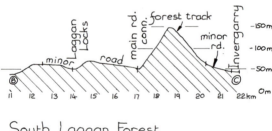

Laggan Locks — minor road — main rd. conn. — forest track — minor rd. — Invergarry (C) — 150m — 100m — 50m — 0m

11 12 13 14 15 16 17 18 19 20 21 22km

South Laggan Forest

Glenfintaig — road — to Glen Gloy — track — Hotel — old railway — 100m — 50m — 0m

0 1 2 3 4 5 6 7 8 9 10 11km

South Laggan — old station — old rly — Gen. Wade's Road — Aber-chalder — 50m — 0m

11 12 13 14 15 16 17 18 19 20 21km

18

The Great Glen Routes 2

Invergarry to Fort Augustus

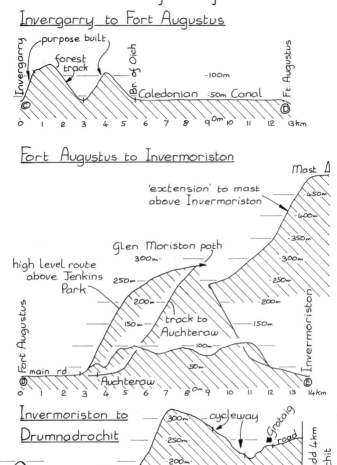

Fort Augustus to Invermoriston

Invermoriston to Drumnadrochit

19

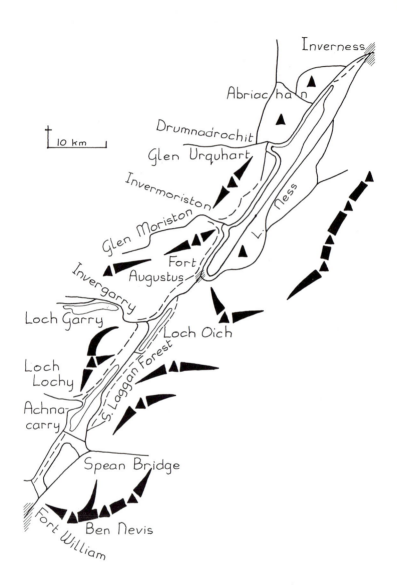

Inverness

Abriachan

Drumnadrochit

Glen Urquhart

Invermoriston

Glen Moriston

Fort
Augustus

Invergarry

Loch Garry

Loch Oich

Loch
Lochy

Achna-
carry

S. Laggan Forest

Spean Bridge

Ben Nevis

Fort William

L. Ness

10 km

The first section of the cycleway is an easy 15km or 10m of level towpath and undulating road. Your author recommends starting from Fort William, as the sight of the town's ugly architecture is a shock after the tranquillity and scenic views of the towpath. Fort William is in a magnificent position at the foot of Britain's highest mountain, yet the planners appear to have imported all that is the very worst of '70s big-city-architecture and incorporated it into the town. We have masses of concrete, a bypass, subways, mono-pitched and flat roofs and garish colours. Litter, vandalism and graffiti follow as the built environment affects behaviour. The result is an unattractive blot where we could have had a beautiful town, with a bit of thought. An opportunity missed! It is soon left behind; the Great Glen Cycle Route (GGCR) runs on the south east side of the canal.

Cont'd Ft.W. to Ach'y 2

327m

B8004

150m

100m

50m

GGCR

R. Lochy

Neptune's Staircase (locks) Start of GGCR at swing br's.

N

1km

this minor road may be used part of the way into Fort William — centre 4km.

Corpach

A830

Banavie

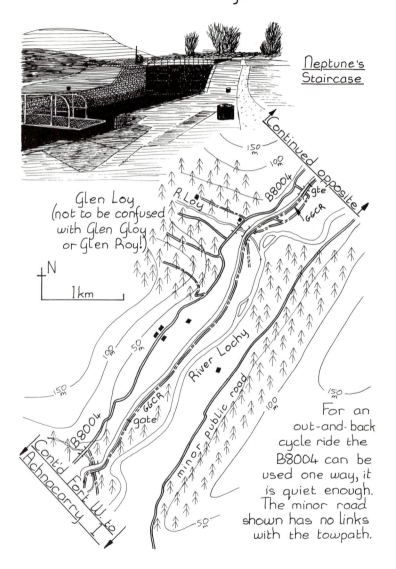

Neptune's Staircase

Continued opposite →

150 m

100 m

B8004

gte

66CR

Glen Loy
(not to be confused
with Glen Gloy
or Glen Roy!)

R. Loy

↑ N

1km

100 m

50 m

150 m

66CR

gate

B8004

River Lochy

minor public road

150 m

100 m

50 m

Cont'd Fort W. to Achnacarry 1 →

For an
out-and-back
cycle ride the
B8004 can be
used one way, it
is quiet enough.
The minor road
shown has no links
with the towpath.

22

Swing Bridge

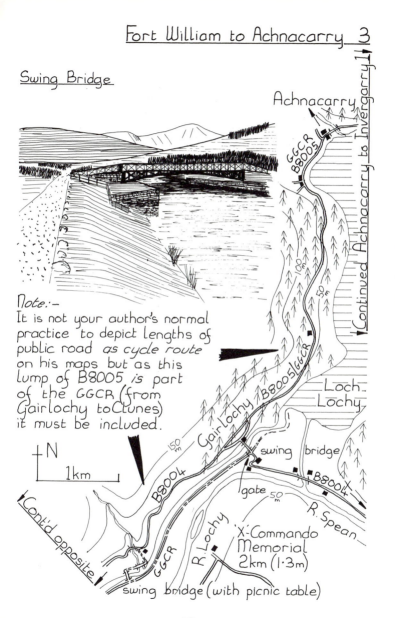

Note:-
It is not your author's normal practice to depict lengths of public road *as cycle route* on his maps but as this lump of B8005 *is* part of the GGCR (from Gairlochy toClunes) it must be included.

N
1km

Achnacarry

Continued Achnacarry to Invergarry 1

GGCR B8005

100m

50m

Loch Lochy

B8005 GGCR

Gairlochy

150m

B8004

swing bridge

B8004

gate 50m

R. Spean

Cont'd opposite

GGCR

R. Lochy

'X'-Commando Memorial
2km (1·3m)

swing bridge (with picnic table)

Achnacarry to Invergarry 1

The Achnacarry to Invergarry section of the GGCR comprises a superb undulating forest track alongside Loch Lochy for some 11km (7m); then a minor road from South Laggan to North Laggan (4km or 2.5m); from which a forest track rises above Loch Oich before dropping finally to Invergarry. The distance from the River Arkaig bridge by Achnacarry is 21km or 13m, or 1.5km (1m) less from the car park at Clunes. Note the picnic spot/car park at Laggan Locks; pedestrians and bikes can cross the canal here. There is no shelter but main road connections exist at North and South Laggan. A further picnic area (and shop) lies 200m up the main road at the south western end of Loch Oich.

645m

588m

runs to a dead end

250m

200m

150m

100m

GGCR

50m

c. grid gate

Lochy

It is difficult to 'pair' this route up with South Laggan Forest without either encroaching on enclosed farmland and private driveways or cycling on the too-busy A82 from Glenfintaig to the Commando Memorial.

Continued opposite

Continued Fort William to Achnacy 3

Clunes

c. grid gate

to Loch Arkaig

car park

GGCR   B8005

Achnacarry
1.5 km / 1m

24

Loch Lochy

N

1km

Sean Mheall 887m

Cont'd Achnacarry to Invergarry 3

Meall Dubh 837m

concrete br.
Glas-dhoire
(ruin)

large and small gates - _and a stile!_

high gate and stile

concrete bridge

Ctd opposite

lg. & sm. gates

It is indeed a pleasure to wander along the quiet side of Loch Lochy whilst those engaged in the rat-race tear along, unseeing, on the main road at the other side of the loch. How driving deprives the senses of the simple pleasures of life!

It is a shame that the welcome extended to walkers and cyclists by Forest Enterprise ⟶ is not shared by other landowners in the area. [Your author has yet to witness the damage a bicycle can allegedly do to a hard-surfaced track.....]

<u>Note:—</u> the chalet park at "X". The dark colours of the chalets are barely visible from across the loch. Thank you. It is so easy to get it right.

<u>Note</u>

It is possible for cyclists and pedestrians to cross the canal at Laggan Locks.

N ↑
1km

Meall nan Dearcag 689m

Kilfinnan Burn

Laggan Locks

road GGCR

A82

Public

Ceann Loch

conc. br.

gate
c.grid • br.

X

c.grid
+ gates

to a dead end

GGCR

Loch Lochy

Continued opposite

Continued South Laggan Forest 4

Continued Achnacarry to Invergarry 2

The Great Glen Cycle route has been easy all the way from Fort William. Now the fun starts with a steep, but thankfully short climb out of Invergarry. The hard-won height is soon lost in returning to the shore of Loch Oich. The tracks around Lochs Garry and Loyne will have to wait a year or three for your author's attention... pity! They look so tempting.

Continued Invergarry to Fort Augustus 1

N
1 km

GGCR
Oich!
100
views
A82
A87
-50
-50 minor road
Invergarry
100
GGCR
views
GGCR
A82
Loch Oich
hotel
cas.

Your author spent his honeymoon here – aaah!

ruin – Glas-dhoire

car park
link path
c-grid
GGCR minor road
Continued South Laggan Forest 4
200
150
100
50
GGCR minor road
A82

Continued opposite

South Laggan Forest 1

South Laggan Forest flanks both sides of Loch Lochy. The north west side is inextricably linked with the Great Glen Cycle Route which includes half of South Laggan Forest and this is covered in the previous section, Achnacarry to Invergarry. This section deals primarily with the Fort William to Fort Augustus railway, between Glenfintaig and Aberchalder. Parts of the route are (or were at the time of my survey) overgrown. The section to Aberchalder is subject to a ban on mountainbikes from about a mile north of the old station at North Laggan. Dogs (and sensibly fires and litter) are also banned. However both the old railway and General Wade's road are of great interest alongside Loch Oich. Note also the old walkers' path from Letterfinlay Lodge Hotel over to the head of Glen Gloy. Total walking distance from Lower Glenfintaig to Aberchalder is 20km or 13miles. The best starting point for mountainbiking (where permitted) is the old station at North Laggan.

Bridge of Oich

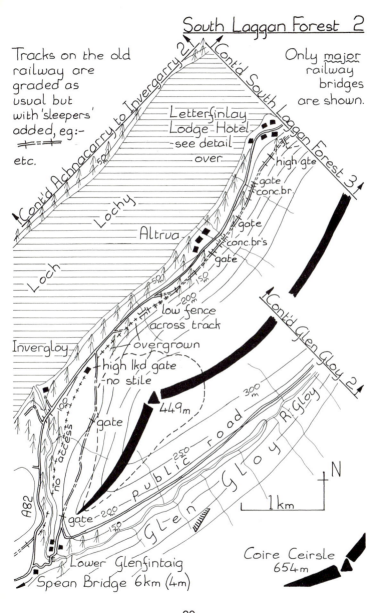

Tracks on the old railway are graded as usual but with 'sleepers' added, eg:-
etc.

Only major railway bridges are shown.

Cont'd to Invergarry 2

Cont'd South Laggan Forest 3

Cont'd Achnacarry to Invergarry 2

Letterfinlay Lodge Hotel
-see detail over.

high gte
gate
conc.br.

Lochy

Altrua

gate
conc.br's
gate

50m
150m
200m

low fence across track

overgrown

Cont'd Glen Gloy 2

Invergloy

high lkd gate
-no stile

449m

300m

no access

gate

Glen Gloy River Gloy

public road

250m
200m
150m

A82

gate

N

1km

Lower Glenfintaig

Spean Bridge 6km (4m)

Coire Ceirsle 654m

29

South Laggan Forest 3

The environs of Letterfinlay Lodge Hotel

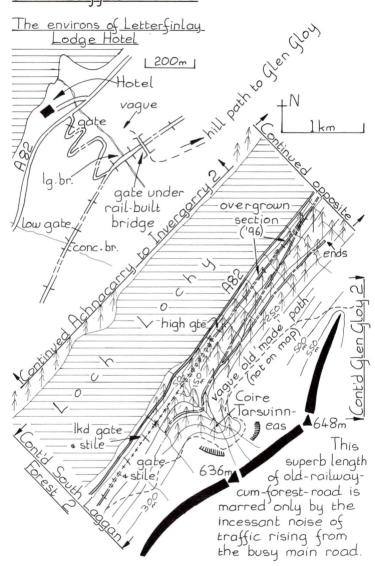

|_ 200m _|

Hotel

vague

gate

A82

lg. br.

low gate

conc. br.

gate under rail-built bridge

hill path to Glen Gloy

N

|_ 1 km _|

Continued opposite

Continued Achnacarry to Invergarry 2

overgrown section ('96)

ends

A82

high gte

Coire Tarsuinn-eas

648m

Cont'd Glen Gloy 2

vague old 'made' path (not on map)

Continued South Laggan Forest 2

lkd gate
stile

gate
stile

636m

This superb length of old-railway-cum-forest-road is marred only by the incessant noise of traffic rising from the busy main road.

The environs of the old station at North Laggan

NO BIKES to the north!

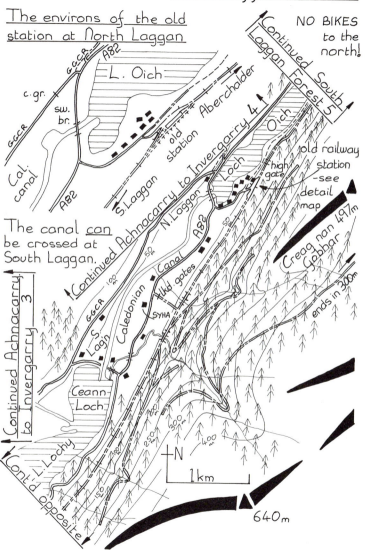

The canal can be crossed at South Laggan.

L. Oich

c.gr.

sw. br.

Cal. canal

A82

G.G.C.R.

A82

S.Laggan

old station

Aberchalder

Continued South Laggan Forest 5

L. Oich

old railway station -see detail map

high gate

N.Laggan

Loch

Creag nan Gobhar 497m

ends in 300m

Continued Achnacarry to Invergarry 4

A82

Caledonian Canal

lkd gates

SYHA

G.G.C.R.

S. Lgn

Ceann-Loch

100m

50m

50m

300m

250m

400m

Continued Achnacarry to Invergarry 3

Cont'd L. Lochy

Cont'd opposite

+N

1km

640m

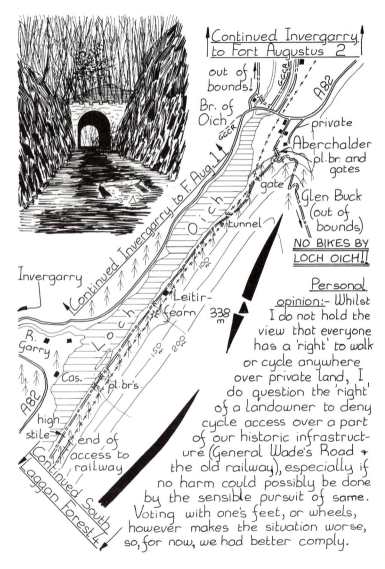

Continued Invergarry to Fort Augustus 2

out of bounds!

Br. of Oich

private

Aberchalder pl. br. and gates

gate

Glen Buck (out of bounds)

NO BIKES BY LOCH OICH!!

Continued Invergarry to F. Aug. 1

Loch Oich

tunnel

Leitir-fearn

338 m

Invergarry

R. Garry

Cas.

pt. brs.

high stile

end of access to railway

A82

100

150 m

200 m

Continued South Laggan Forest 4

Personal opinion:- Whilst I do not hold the view that everyone has a 'right' to walk or cycle anywhere over private land, I do question the 'right' of a landowner to deny cycle access over a part of our historic infrastructure (General Wade's Road & the old railway), especially if no harm could possibly be done by the sensible pursuit of same. Voting with one's feet, or wheels, however makes the situation worse, so, for now, we had better comply.

This section of the Great Glen Cycle Route comprises a steep climb on a purpose built cycle path out of Invergarry, a descending forest road, then a further purpose built section to Aberchalder. The scene changes for the remainder of the way to Fort Augustus, along the canal towpath. The Invergarry to Aberchalder section is time consuming in comparison with the fast ride up the smooth towpath. The total distance from Invergarry to Fort Augustus is 13·5km (8·5m) of which 8km (5m) is on the towpath. There is no shelter, nor is there an alternative for a return via the minor road and forest tracks as the Invervigar Burn bridge no longer exists and bikes are banned around Loch Lundie.

204m Bridge of Oich (see detail over)

purpose built cycle path

GGCR

N

1 km

Invergarry :- 'phone box, loo, parking, shop etc..

212m

GGCR

GGCR

100

50

Loch

Oich

hotel

Castle

GGCR

Continued South Laggan Forest 5

Cont'd Invergarry to Fort Augustus 2

Cont'd Achnacarry to Invergarry 4

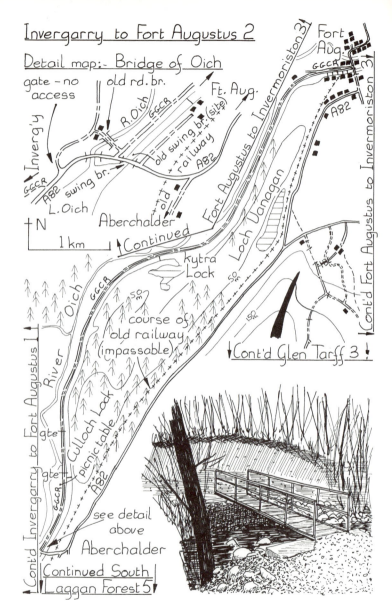

Detail map:- Bridge of Oich

gate – no access

old rd. br.

Ft. Aug.

Fort Aug.

GGCR

R. Oich

GGCR

Inverg'y

A82

L. Oich

swing br.

old swing br. (site)

railway

A82

old

Aberchalder

Fort Augustus to Invermoriston 3

Fort Augustus to Invermoriston 3

A82

Loch Uanagan

Cont'd Fort Augustus to Invermoriston 3

N

1 km

Continued

Kytra Lock

50 m

50 m

150 m

Cont'd Glen Tarff 3

River Oich

GGCR

course of old railway (impassable)

Culloch Lock

picnic table

A82

GGCR

gte

gte

Cont'd Invergarry to Fort Augustus 1

Fort Augustus 1

see detail above

Aberchalder

Continued South
Laggan Forest 5

The Fort Augustus to Invermoriston section of the Great Glen Cycle Route offers variations at either end, extending considerably the scope for cycling out and back as not all has to be repeated. The south western end may be extended to the Invervigar Burn and Auchteraw Wood and the high level track above Jenkins Park is excellent though not a part of the official GGCR. At the north eastern end the track climbs to the mast above Invermoriston - a fine viewpoint for Loch Ness. The direct (GGCR) distance from Fort Augustus is 14km or 9 miles. The Invervigar Burn adds about 16km (10m) return, and the trip up to the mast a further 20km (12m) return. There is no shelter but rescue is at hand in the various cafes in Fort Augustus and the hotel at Invermoriston. The above options, the GGCR to Invergarry, and Glen Tarff (for the Corrie-airack Pass) add up to making Fort Augustus a good centre for mountainbiking - and of course walking – limited only by the restrictions imposed by Aberchalder Estate.

The high level track

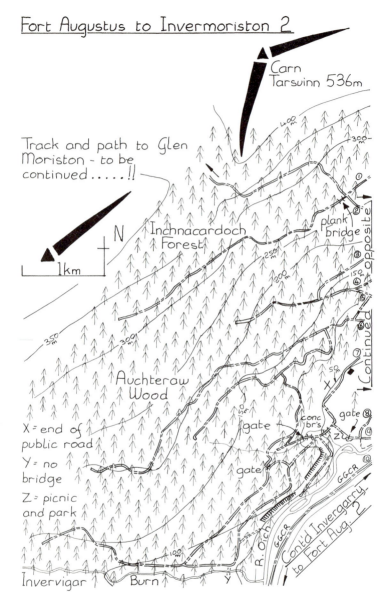

Carn Tarsuinn 536m

Track and path to Glen Moriston - to be continued .....!!

1km

N

Inchnacardoch Forest

plank bridge

Continued opposite

Auchteraw Wood

X = end of public road

Y = no bridge

Z = picnic and park

gate

gate

conc br's

gate

Continued

Invervigar   Burn

R. Oich

GGCR

GGCR

Cont'd Invergarry - to Fort Aug. 2

High level alternative to the GGCR
providing extensive views and
avoiding the short length
of main road
at X-X

Cont'd F.Aug. to Itton 4

GGCR

gate Z

X

bridge
on old road;
parking, walks.

A82/GGCR

X

Loch Ness

Jenkins Park

conc. brs.

Fort Augustus

GGCR

high gates

lkd gate no go!

Y

R Tarff

old railway

N

1km

B862

This is a
minor road route
to Inverness -up
a huge hill - but
avoiding the Drum.
to Inverness main
trunk road.

gravel pit

R Oich

Loch Uanagan

GGCR

50 m

Cont'd opposite

Cont'd Invergarry to Ft. Augustus 2

A82

↓Continued Glen Tarff 3↓

Y = parking and forest walks

Z = this must be the Forest Enterprise
entry for "The most complicated
gate in Scotland" competition!

Fort Augustus to Invermoriston 4

Your author apologises for his infantile drawing of
the Loch Ness Monster — the detail of the last
two pages has taken its toll!

↑Continued opposite↑

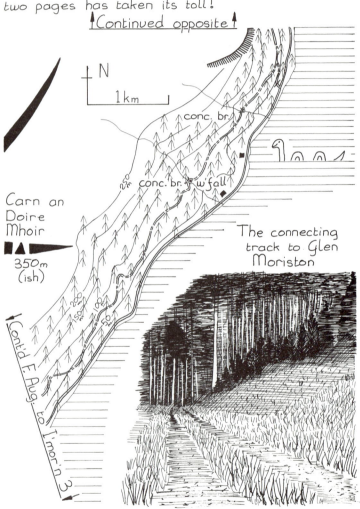

N

1 km

conc. br.

conc. br. w'fall

Carn an
Doire
Mhoir

350m
(ish)

200
150
100
50

Contd F. Aug. to I'morin 3

The connecting
track to Glen
Moriston

Continued Invermoriston to Drumnadrochit 1

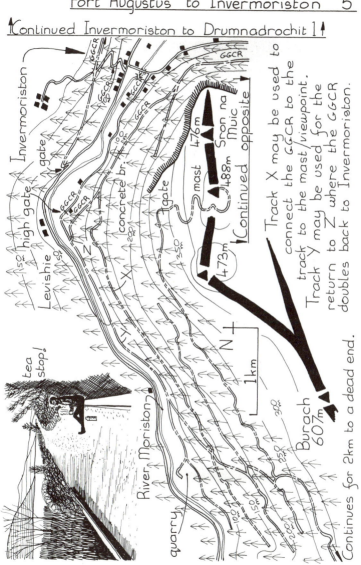

Invermoriston

GGCR

high gate

gate

Levishie

GGCR

concrete br.

gate

mast

476m

488m

Sron na Muic
Continued opposite

473m

tea stop!

River Moriston

quarry

Burgach 607m

N

1km

Track X may be used to connect the GGCR to the track to the mast/viewpoint. Track Y may be used for the return to Z where the GGCR doubles back to Invermoriston.

Continues for 2km to a dead end.

39

Invermoriston to Drumnadrochit 1

The 20km or 12·5mile final section of the Great Glen Cycle Route ends at Drumnadrochit. After visiting Urquhart Castle (the approach by bike being perilous) there remain two choices of road route into Inverness. The "official" route is to climb the hill over to the head of Glen Convinth, thence on minor roads via Abriachan reaching the A82 about 5km (3m) from Inverness. Your author's recommendation is to go via Glen Urquhart to Cannich (SYHA hostel and good off road cycling) thence via the quiet side of Strathglass and Beauly. The route from Invermoriston to Drum' is part forest track, part purpose made mountainbike track and part road. There is a considerable amount of climbing. Shelter is available at the Stone Cave.

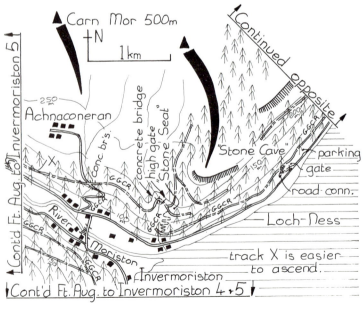

Continued opposite

Contd Ft. Aug. to Invermoriston 5

Cont'd Ft. Aug. to Invermoriston 4 + 5

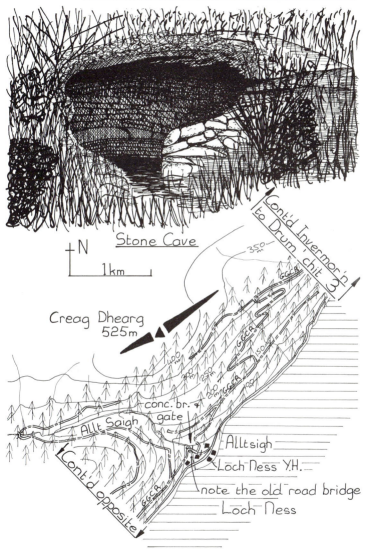

Stone Cave

N
1km

Creag Dhearg
525m

Cont'd Invermor'n to Drum'chit 3

350 m

400 m
300 m
250 m
200 m

conc. br.
gate

Allt Saigh

Cont'd opposite

G.G.C.R

Alltsigh
Loch Ness Y.H.
note the old road bridge
Loch Ness

Invermoriston to Drumnadrochit 3

The Environs of Grotaig

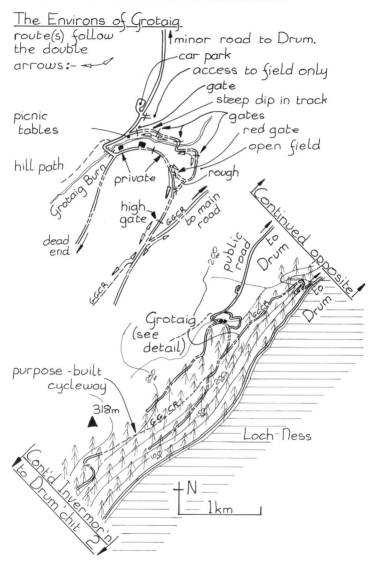

route(s) follow the double arrows:-

minor road to Drum.
car park
access to field only
gate
steep dip in track
gates
red gate
open field

picnic tables

hill path

Grotaig Burn

private

rough

high gate

dead end

GGCR

to main road

GGCR

Continued opposite

public road

to Drum

to Drum

200m

Grotaig (see detail)

GGCR

purpose-built cycleway

200m

318m

GGCR

150m
200m

Loch Ness

100m

Cont'd Invermor'n to Drum'chit 2

N

1km

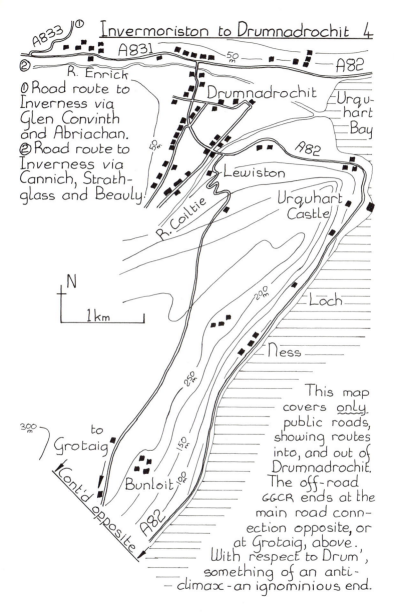

A833

A831

R. Enrick

50 m

A82

① Road route to Inverness via Glen Convinth and Abriachan.

② Road route to Inverness via Cannich, Strathglass and Beauly.

Drumnadrochit

Urquhart Bay

50 m

A82

Lewiston

R. Coiltie

Urquhart Castle

N

1 km

200 m

Loch

Ness

250 m

300 m

to Grotaig

Cont'd opposite

150 m

Bunloit

100 m

A82

This map covers only public roads, showing routes into, and out of Drumnadrochit. The off-road GGCR ends at the main road connection opposite, or at Grotaig, above. With respect to Drum', something of an anticlimax - an ignominious end.

43

South West Monadhliath

South West Monadhliath

Access:— The south west end of the remote Monadhliath mountains is accessible from Fort William; either via the A82 for the Great Glen or via the A86 for Glen Spean, both via Spean Bridge. The glens fall conveniently into two pairs and all are linked, though the Glen Roy to Glen Gloy link is somewhat tenuous and suitable for walkers only. The proximity of the Great Glen Cycle Route and Leanachan Forest, Strath Ossian etc. (Book 3) make the Spean Bridge/Roybridge area an excellent centre with the added advantage of train services heading for Fort William.

Accommodation:— SYHA Hostels at Glen Nevis and Loch Lochy supplement the many B+Bs in the Roybridge area. Private bunkhouses and camping are also available. The tourist info. centres in Fort William (open all year) and Spean Bridge (Apr. to Oct.) will advise.

Geographical Features:— A high mountain area deeply intersected by the Glen Roy to Spey Head glens. South east of this divide lies the Creag Meagaidh range of mountains - and no other significant long glens. The lesser, more rounded heights in the north and west of the region are very wild and, not being Munros, only seldom visited. The so-called parallel roads of Glen Gloy and Glen Roy are the remains of the shorelines of a vast ice-dammed lake (loch?), held back at three different levels for the actions of wind and waves to erode the hillsides and leave evidence of the power of ice, wind and water for all to see.

Mountains:— The mountain mass of Creag Meagaidh dominates the south of the region, with its many subsidiary summits, corries and

a complex system of connecting ridges. This is
an area for the experienced walker and winter
mountaineer only. The hills to the north of the
region are of little individual interest yet
collectively they form one of our most precious
assets, in maintaining a wilderness area. It is
from the north that the lover of these wild
places will approach Creag Meagaidh - not for
him (or her) the 'tourist' path.

Rivers:- Always a more prominent feature in an
area of such high rainfall. The heart of the region
gives rise to the Spey whilst the River Roy and
River Gloy head west to Spean and Lochy. The
River Tarff heads east via Loch Ness. There are
no major river crossings other than the Turret
which may have to be followed downstream to
Turret Bridge; and the Allt Chonnal, behind Luib-
chonnal bothy in Glen Roy which may be difficult
to cross when in spate.

Forests:- One side of Glen Gloy is planted, spoiling not only the appearance of the glen but
destroying part of the old path over to Glen Roy.
Spey Head is also marred by random blocks of
forest apparently planned to be as un-natural as
possible in their visual impact.

Lochs:- None, though Loch Lochy and Loch
Laggan border the area. The only other significant loch is the tiny Loch Spey - the source
of this fine salmon river.

Emergency:- The wildness of the Corrieyairack
Pass and the Roy/Spey watershed is not to be
under-estimated. The bothies at Luib-chonnal
and Melgarve provide shelter but there is no
habitation between Brae Roy Lodge in Glen Roy,
Upper Glenfintaig in Glen Gloy, Culachy House
in Glen Tarff and Garvamore above Spey Dam.
Between these points you are very much on your
own - care please - and watch the weather!

South West Monadhliath Routes 1

Glen Roy.

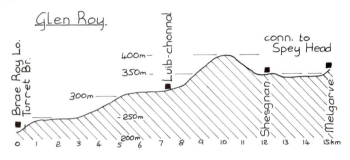

Glen Tarff.

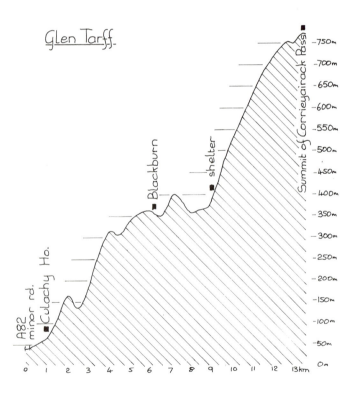

Glen Gloy.

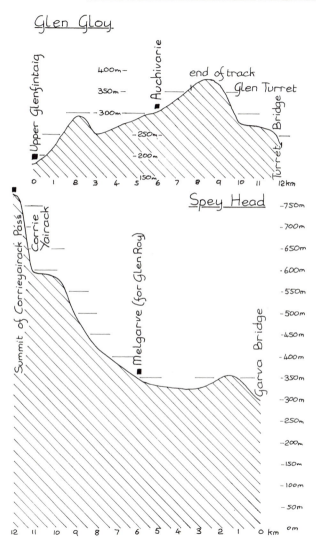

Spey Head

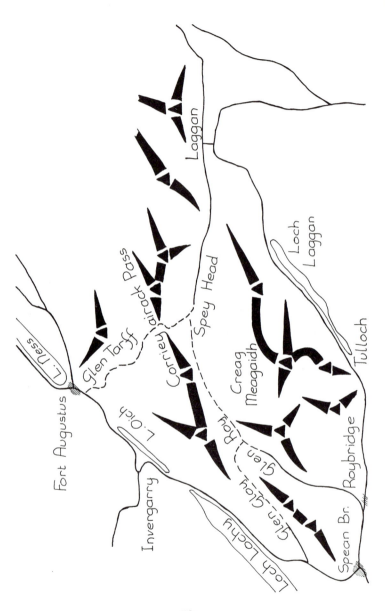

50

Glen Roy 1

Glen Roy is divisible into three sections. Firstly, the metalled road from Roybridge to Brae Roy Lodge - a public road (and therefore not on the maps over) but an excellent prelude to cycling the rather short 'track' section of the glen. Thirdly a path runs from the end of the track at Luib-chonnal bothy to Shesgnan. Though a walkers' path this section is possibly justifiable with a bike as part of a longer tour. After Shesgnan a track is joined connecting this with the Corrieyairack Pass. The col, a mile or so past the bothy reveals Loch Spey, the source of this fine river. A tenuous connection exists to Glen Gloy, and therefore South Laggan Forest. The O.S. map is confusing as the "parallel roads" (not roads at all but the shorelines of glacial lakes) are depicted as an "unfenced other road, drive or track" - strange! There is shelter at the bothy. Distances are as set out below. Views are superb throughout.

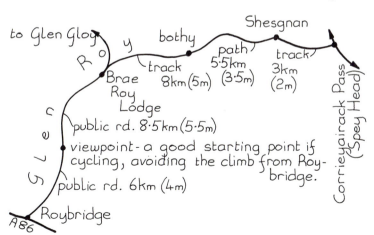

to Glen Gloy

Shesgnan

bothy

R o y

track

path 5·5km (3·5m)

track 3km (2m)

Brae Roy Lodge

track 8km (5m)

Corrieyairack Pass (Spey Head)

public rd. 8·5km (5·5m)

viewpoint - a good starting point if cycling, avoiding the climb from Roybridge.

public rd. 6km (4m)

Roybridge

A86

Glen Roy 2

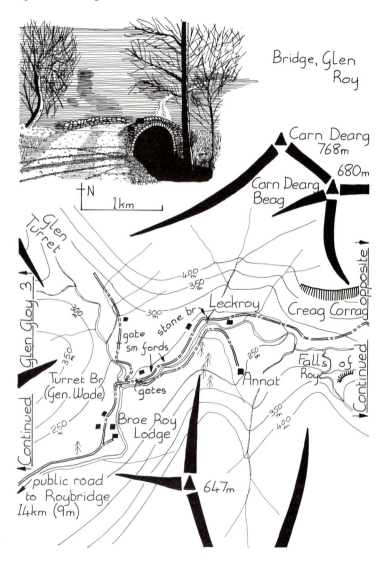

Bridge, Glen Roy

Carn Dearg 768m

680m

Carn Dearg Beag

Glen Turret

Glen Gloy 3

400 m
350 m

Leckroy

Creag Corrag

300

300

stone br.

gate
sm. fords

250 m

Falls of Roy

Turret Br.
(Gen. Wade)

gates

250 m

Annat

Brae Roy Lodge

350 m
400 m

647m

← Continued Glen Gloy 3

← Continued

opposite →

Continued →

public road to Roybridge 14km (9m)

N   1km

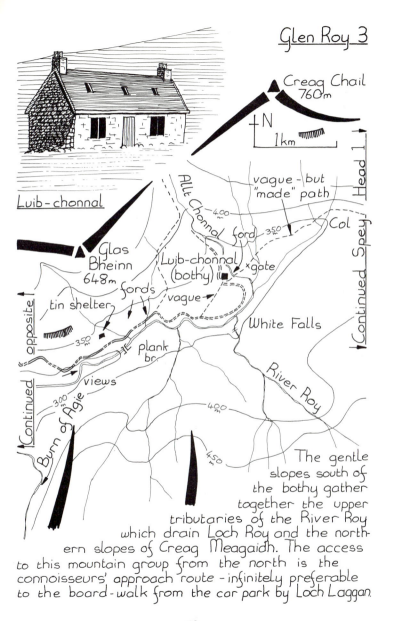

Creag Chail
760m

N

1km

vague - but "made" path

Allt Chonnal

Head 1

ford

400

350m

Col

Luib-chonnal

Glas Bheinn
648m

Luib-chonnal (bothy)

x gate

Continued Spey

fords

vague

tin shelter

opposite!

350m

White Falls

plank br.

Continued

views

River Roy

300m

Burn of Agie

400m

450m

The gentle slopes south of the bothy gather together the upper tributaries of the River Roy which drain Loch Roy and the northern slopes of Creag Meagaidh. The access to this mountain group from the north is the connoisseurs' approach route - infinitely preferable to the board-walk from the car park by Loch Laggan.

Glen Gloy 1

The geographical similarities and proximity of Glen Gloy and Glen Roy invite comparison. Glen Gloy is the poor relation. Its steep sides and planted forest conspire in shutting out the views. Not here the open aspects of neighbouring Glen Roy. Even the parallel "roads" are not so obvious. An ancient highway used to pass through to Glen Roy. This has now been omitted from the O.S. maps despite much beyond the col being traceable. Some 400m before the col has been destroyed by planting. The omission of the mapped record is surely the death-knell for these ancient routes as few will seek out what is not on the present-day map. Who indeed has the right to decide this old highway has ceased to exist ? We are not allowed to destroy our old buildings - these old tracks are also a part of our heritage.....

The forest road extends some 8km (5m) from the end of the public road at Upper Glenfintaig to the turn-around. The continuation is only practicable on foot which is a pity as this puts cyclists wishing to complete Link Route 2 on the main road to Roybridge. There is no shelter, Auchivarie is private and locked.

The environs of Upper Glenfintaig.

end of public road

best route

gates

becomes very rough

gates

Upper Glenfintaig

The addition of the public road from Glenfintaig adds some 5km or 3m for cyclists after a vicious climb!

The vague path at X continues around
the head of Coire Tarsuinn-eas and
descends to the Letterfinlay Lodge
Hotel via the rail-built bridge over
the old railway shown on South
Laggan Forest 3 . (The bridge
with the gate under it). This
path is not on the 1:50000
O.S. map but is on the
1:25 000 map. This is a
useful link for walkers
wishing to shorten the
circuit given as Link
Route 2.

Leitir Fhionnlaigh 648m

Druim Ghlaoidh 636m

Cont'd S.Lag.For.3

Continued Glen Gloy 3

X

Achivarie
gates

Alltnara (ruin)
high gate
plank bridge
high gate

high gate

Upper Glenfintaig (see detail opp.)

high gate

Beinn
larvinn 803m

N

1km

Beith Og
595m

Glen

Fintaig

Glen Gloy 3

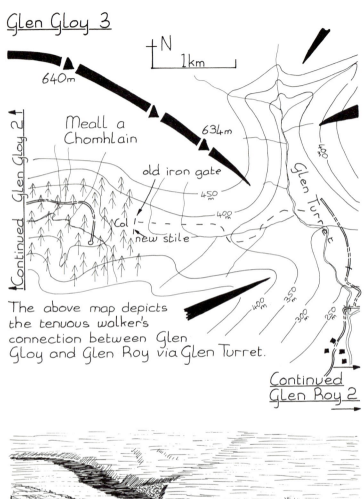

N
1km

640m

Meall a Chomhlain

634m

old iron gate

450 m

400 m

Col

new stile

Glen Turret

400 m

Continued Glen Gloy 2 →

The above map depicts the tenuous walker's connection between Glen Gloy and Glen Roy via Glen Turret.

400 m   350 m   300 m   250 m

Continued Glen Roy 2 →

The Corrieyairack Pass (Glen Tarff plus Spey Head) enjoys, or perhaps suffers, the status of a public road. Originally one of General Wade's roads, complete with interesting bridges, this route has for many years been used by four-wheel-drive enthusiasts. This caused much damage to the track leaving sections extremely rough. However, a flood has now washed out the Fort Augustus end and its use as a through road is impossible. Long may this situation remain as, apart from essential estate use, vehicles should not be permitted in such a wild place. These wilderness areas need fiercely defending if the unrelenting progress of the motor vehicle is to be halted, preferably before the last remnants of our wild country are spoilt. It is often argued that the conservation of wilderness is selfish in denying access to those unable, or just not fit enough to walk or cycle into these areas. Conservation for future generations cannot surely be selfish? The further development of road access (and mountain railway/chair-lift/funicular etc.) destroys the very essence of the environment we wish to enjoy.... Your author is a poor swimmer and cannot (nay, dare not!) dive, yet he does not expect a part of the ocean to be drained so that he may inspect the coral reef on foot, or by car! By the same token, wilderness areas must never be destroyed by the lazy man's means of access. If you cannot get up the mountain because you are unfit, or to the coral because you can't swim — tough! That is what photography is for. Look at the pictures. No one has the right to destroy what

Glen Tarff 2 (Corrieyairack Pass)

he seeks to enjoy - merely to make access easy. I digress - this is supposed to be a guide to the Corrieyairack Pass - not an essay!! The track at the Fort Augustus side is better than the Spey Head approach though there is considerably more climbing. The route is high and exposed, some 25km (16m) from the A82 to Garva Bridge with a total of some 900m of climbing from the Fort Augustus end and about 500m (in total) from Garva Bridge. There is (spartan) emergency shelter at the concrete hut on the climb out of Glen Tarff and at Melgarve bothy. A walkers' path branches off at Melgarve (starting off as a track) heading for Glen Roy. Brae Roy Lodge is 22km or 14m from Garva Bridge. Thanks to General Wade, the route is punctuated by interesting bridges, indeed the route would not exist without the General.

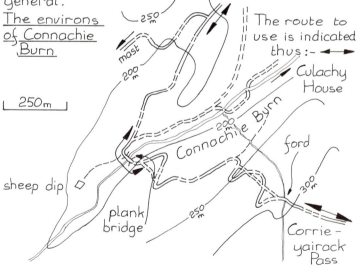

The environs of Connachie Burn

The route to use is indicated thus :- ◄──►

250m

sheep dip

plank bridge

Culachy House

Connachie Burn

ford

Corrie-yairack Pass

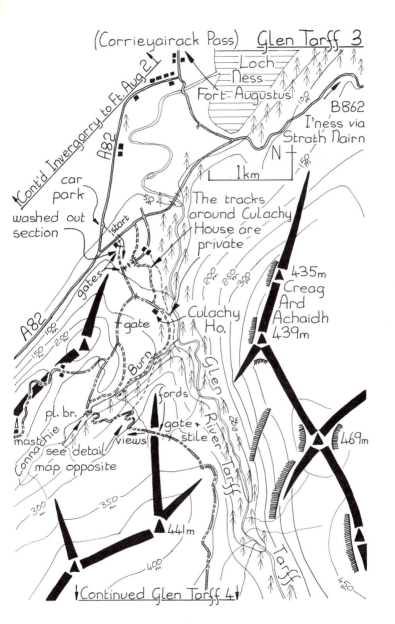

Loch Ness

Fort Augustus

B862
I'ness via
Strath Nairn

Cont'd Invergarry to Ft. Aug. 21

A82

car park

washed out section

The tracks around Culachy House are private

1km

N

start

gates

A82

Culachy Ho.

435m
Creag Ard Achaidh
439m

gate

Burn

469m

fords

gate
stile
views

pl. br.

mastchie
Connachie see detail
map opposite

Glen River Tarff

441m

Continued Glen Tarff 4

Tarff

Glen Tarff 4 (Corrieyairack Pass)

↑Continued Glen Tarff 3↑

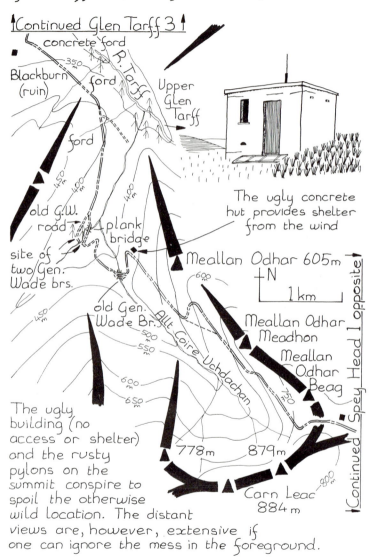

concrete ford

R. Tarff

Blackburn (ruin)

ford

Upper Glen Tarff

350

400m

ford

450m

400m

400m

old G.W. road

plank bridge

site of two Gen. Wade brs.

450m

old Gen. Wade Br.

Allt Coire Uchdachan

500

550

600

650

The ugly concrete hut provides shelter from the wind

Meallan Odhar 605m

+N

1 km

600

Meallan Odhar Meadhon

Meallan Odhar Beag

750

The ugly building (no access or shelter) and the rusty pylons on the summit conspire to spoil the otherwise wild location. The distant views are, however, extensive if one can ignore the mess in the foreground.

778m

879m

Carn Leac 884m

800

←Continued / Spey Head 1 opposite→

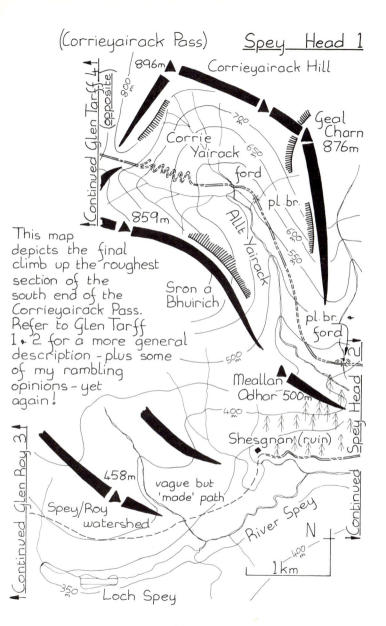

Corrieyairack Hill

896m

Continued Glen Tarff 1+1 (opposite)

800m

Geal Charn 876m

Corrie Yairack

700

650m

ford

pl. br.

Allt Yairack

600m

859m

550m

This map depicts the final climb up the roughest section of the south end of the Corrieyairack Pass. Refer to Glen Tarff 1 + 2 for a more general description - plus some of my rambling opinions - yet again!

Sron a Bhuirich

pl. br. ford

500m

Continued Spey Head 2

Meallan Odhar 500m

400

Shesgnan (ruin)

Continued Glen Roy 3

458m

Spey/Roy watershed

vague but 'made' path

River Spey

N

Continued Spey Head 2

400m

1 km

350m

Loch Spey

Spey Head 2 (Corrieyairack Pass)

It is possible to drive almost to Melgarve but,
despite the metalled road this constitutes the
intrusive use of a car. It is more appropriate to
park at Garva Bridge and proceed on foot or
by bike and thus fully appreciate the upper
Spey - and how this otherwise wild glen has
been marred by lumps of
straight-edged forest
planted at random.

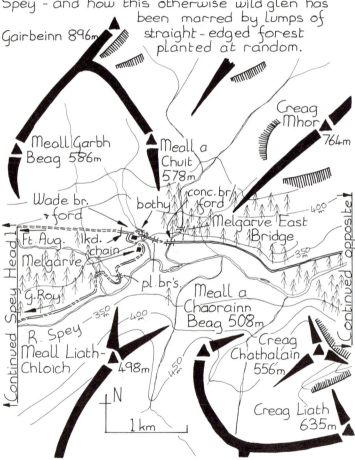

Gairbeinn 896m

Creag Mhor 764m

Meall Garbh Beag 586m

Meall a Chuit 578m

Wade br. ford

bothy

conc. br. ford

Melgarve East Bridge

Ft. Aug. lkd. chain

Melgarve

G. Roy

pl. br's.

Meall a Chaorainn Beag 508m

R. Spey

Meall Liath-Chloich 498m

Creag Chathalain 556m

Creag Liath 635m

400m

350m

350m

400m

450m

Continued Spey Head

Continued opposite

N

1 km

<u>Garva Bridge</u>

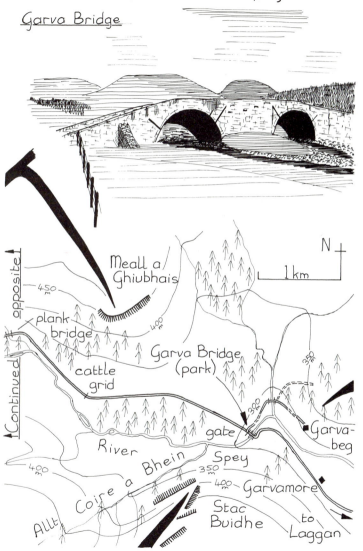

Meall a Ghiubhais

450m

400m

plank bridge

cattle grid

Garva Bridge (park)

350m

opposite

Continued

River

Coire a Bhein

Spey

gate

300m

Garva-beg

Garvamore

400m

350m

400m

Stac Buidhe

Allt

to Laggan

N

1 km

North East Monadhliath

North East Monadhliath

Access:- The access to all the many tracks in this section is from Strath Spey between Spey Dam, above Laggan to Boat of Garten, then north along the A9 to Tomatin. Thankfully the A9 can be avoided everywhere except a short section north of Slochd (where a cycleway is planned) and all routes are linked by minor or secondary roads. Good rail connections to Aviemore, and the variety of routes east of the A9 (Book 1, The Cairngorm Glens) make Aviemore an excellent centre if you don't mind the crowds.

Accommodation:- Hotels, B+Bs, youth hostel, camping etc. all centre on Aviemore. Some further accommodation (mainly B+B) may be found at Kingussie, Newtonmore and Boat of Garten. The all-year-open tourist information centre at Aviemore will assist together with centres at Ralia (on the A9 -open April-Oct) and Kingussie (May - Sept.)

Geographical Features :- This vast area of the Monadhliath Mountains is penetrated only by minor roads up the Findhorn and a short way up the River Dulnain, beyond which it is the province of the adventurous walker and off-road cyclist. Much of the region is remote deer forest and grouse moor so a reminder must be included to respect the stalking and shooting seasons during which time access is restricted to rights of way only (with due consideration being given to estate activities) or elsewhere with permission only. It is obviously better to visit this region outwith the stalking and shooting seasons.

Mountains:- An area of rounded grouse moors with few high mountains other than a small collection of Munros north west of Laggan and Newtonmore. Geal Charn at 926m lies above Glen Markie (Spey Dam) and Carn Ban (942m), Carn Dearg (945m); and Carn Sgulain and A'Chailleach at 920 and 930m lie in an irregular ridge separating the headwaters of the Findhorn from the Spey. The sheer desolation of the heart of this region is the main attraction; not here the tame forest tracks of The Great Glen and Moray. If you seek company, stay in Aviemore!

Rivers:- The region drains to the north east courtesy of the Findhorn, Dulnain and Spey. The Findhorn makes its picturesque way to the sea at Findhorn Bay (see Culbin Forest). The Dulnain joins forces with the Spey at Dulnain Bridge before continuing north and east to Spey Bay. Odd man out is the River Killin which drains Glen Markie (Findhorn) to become the R. Fechlin and R. Foyers, bound for Loch Ness. The Findhorn/Markie watershed is the only (glen) route to the west. The north of the area is drained by the River Nairn.

Forests:- The only significant area of forest provides us with the tracks north of Aviemore linking up with Slochd and the Dulnain. This complex area of tracks together with General Wade's road are a safe bet during the stalking seasons.

Lochs:- None of any great extent. Loch Insh is a bird reserve.

Emergency:- With the exception of the lower Findhorn none of the glens featured has any perm-anent habitation and most are at a *minimum* height of some 300m. Hill tracks rise to around 700m. This is one of the coldest regions in Britain and full consideration should be given to the weather before setting out. You have been warned!!

North East Monadhliath Routes 1

Glen Markie (Findhorn)

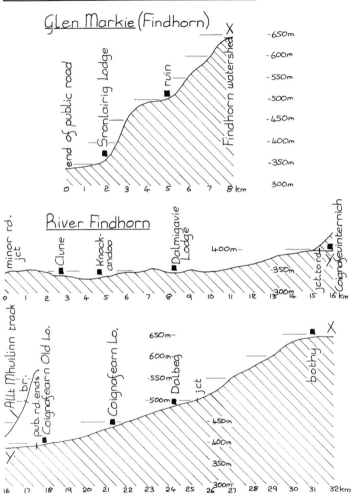

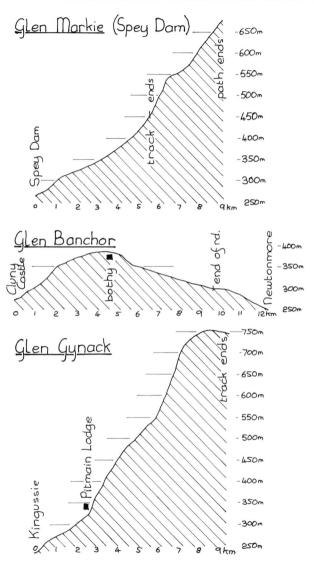

Glen Markie (Spey Dam)

Spey Dam · track · ends · path ends

650m · 600m · 550m · 500m · 450m · 400m · 350m · 300m · 250m

0 1 2 3 4 5 6 7 8 9km

Glen Banchor

Cluny Castle · bothy · end of rd. · Newtonmore

400m · 350m · 300m · 250m

0 1 2 3 4 5 6 7 8 9 10 11 12km

Glen Gynack

Kingussie · Pitmain Lodge · track ends

750m · 700m · 650m · 600m · 550m · 500m · 450m · 400m · 350m · 300m · 250m

0 1 2 3 4 5 6 7 8 9km

North East Monadhliath Routes 3

Raitts Burn

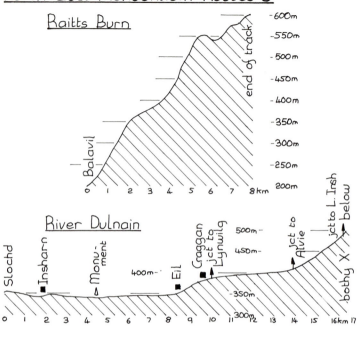

Balavil · end of track

River Dulnain

Slochd · Insharn · Monument · Eil · Craggan · jct to Lynwilg · jct to Alvie · jct to L. Insh below · bothy X

Dulnain to Loch Insh

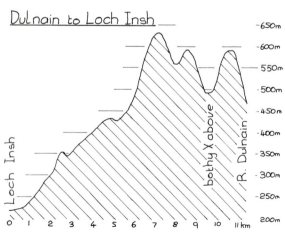

Loch Insh · bothy X above · R. Dulnain

North East Monodhliath Routes 4

Dulnain to Alvie

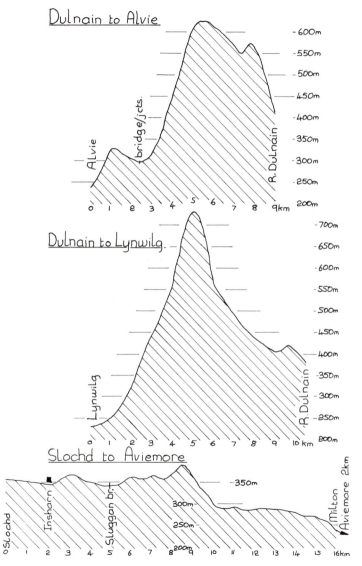

Dulnain to Lynwilg.

Slochd to Aviemore

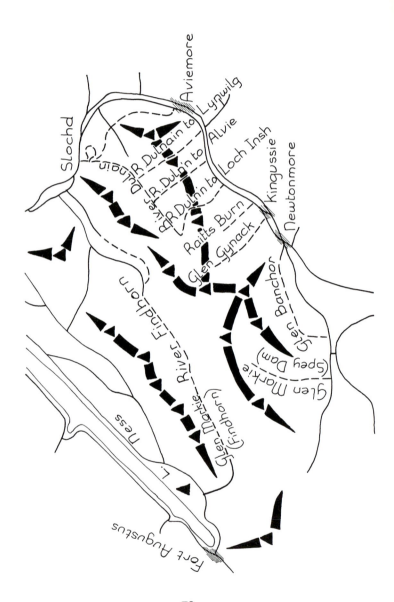

Aviemore

Lynwilg

R Dulnain to Alvie

R Dulnain to Loch Insh

R Dulnain

Slochd

Dulnain

Kingussie

Newtonmore

Raitts Burn

Glen Gynack

Glen Banchor

Glen Markie
(Spey Dam)

Glen Markie
River Findhorn

Glen Markie
(Findhorn)

L. Ness

Fort Augustus

(Findhorn) <u>Glen Markie 1</u>

Glen Markie connects the Findhorn, and therefore the nort east Monadhliath, with Fort Augustus, via General Wade's road, the B862. The public road is signposted Killin from Whitebridge and this ends near Killin Lodge from which a track runs to the ghostly remains of Sronlairig Lo. From here a walkers' path, *vague but "made"* and not shown on the O.S. maps runs up the glen, over the watershed at 650m to the Findhorn. Glen Markie is a superb, wild glen; the watershed is 9km (6m) from the road end.

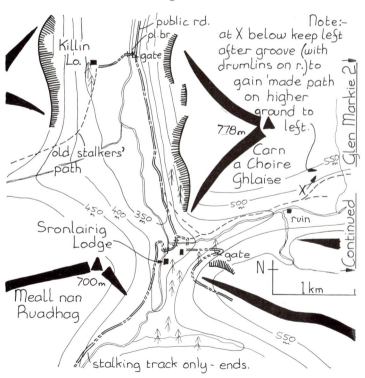

public rd.
pl. br.
Note:-
at X below keep left after groove (with drumlins on r.) to gain 'made' path on higher ground to left.

Killin Lo.
gate

778 m

Carn a Choire Ghlaise

Glen Markie 2

550 m

old stalkers' path

X

500 m

450 400 350

ruin

Sronlairig Lodge

gate

Continued

N

1 km

700 m

Meall nan Ruadhag

550

550

stalking track only - ends.

Glen Markie 2 (Findhorn)

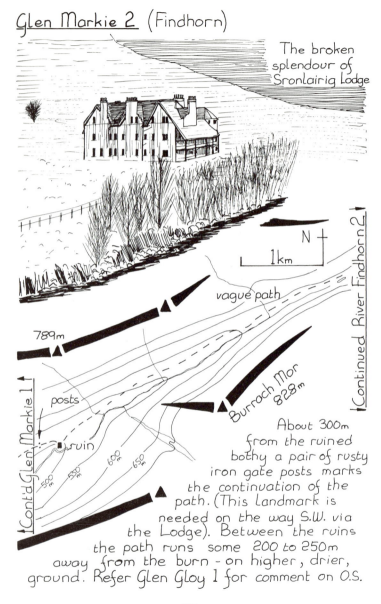

The broken splendour of Sronlairig Lodge

N

1km

vague path

789m

posts

Burrach Mor 828m

ruin

500m 550m 600m 650m

Cont'd Glen Markie 1

Continued River Findhorn 2

About 300m from the ruined bothy a pair of rusty iron gate posts marks the continuation of the path. (This landmark is needed on the way S.W. via the Lodge). Between the ruins the path runs some 200 to 250m away from the burn - on higher, drier, ground. Refer Glen Gloy 1 for comment on O.S.

The River Findhorn drains much of the central
Monadhliath mountains, flowing from the remote
heart of this mountain region and continuing
on its beautiful and ever-changing course to
Findhorn Bay, beyond Culbin Forest. The river
rises in an unfrequented area of heather
clad moorland, devoid even of attractive
peaks - and the people they attract. This area
is true wilderness; its appeal lies only in its
remoteness. If, dear reader, you want to be
alone to contemplate the meaning of life, the
source of the River Findhorn is the place to
be..... The route is divided into two
sections, the lower, from Findhorn Bridge
runs parallel with the public road for some
15km (9·5m) culminating in a side track up the
Allt a Mhuilin (worth seeing as far as the
bridge). A complex obstacle course (see
detail map) gains the public road for 2km
before the track continues for a further 14km
(9m) to the bothy. A pathless connection
continues via Glen Markie to Fort Augustus,
some 66 km or 41miles from Tomatin. The best
bet on a bike is to head up the glen by the
tracks, walking the final half mile or so to
the bothy, returning by the upper track,
then by the quiet public
road down the lower
glen, an out-and-back
ride of 63 km or 39
miles. There is shelter
only at the bothy which
was in a poor state of
repair on your author's
visit in October '95.

The bothy

Carn Gearresith 725m

710m

sm. ford

650m

head of Glenmarkie Burn

Glen Markie 2

650m

Continued opposite

River Eskin w'falls

650m

bothy

700m

Carn na Saobhaidh

Carn Coire na Creiche 826m

Continued

N

1 km

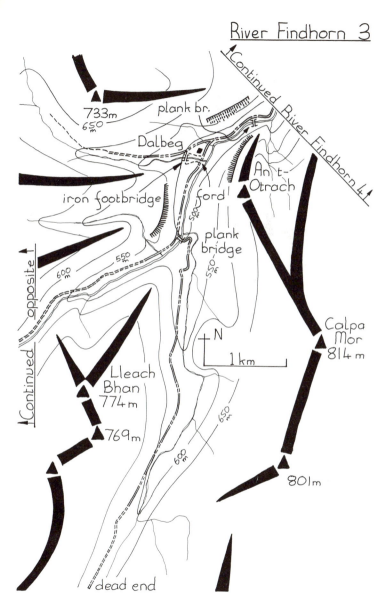

Continued River Findhorn 4

Continued opposite

733m
650m

plank br.

Dalbeg

iron footbridge

ford

500m

plank bridge

550m

An t-Otrach

600m
550m

N
1 km

Calpa Mor
814 m

Lleach Bhan
774 m

769m

650m
600m

801m

dead end

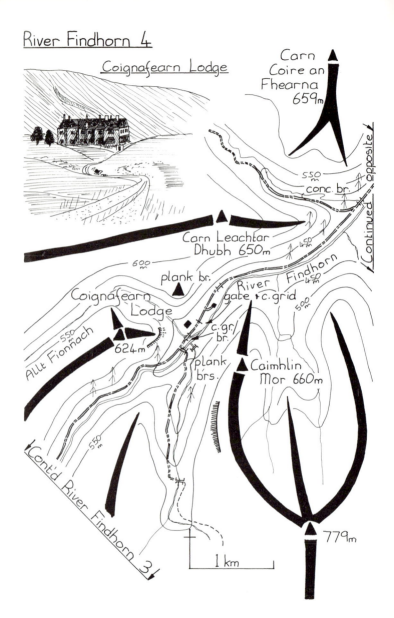

Coignafearn Lodge

Carn Coire an Fhearna 659m

conc. br.

Carn Leachtar Dhubh 650m

plank br.

Coignafearn Lodge

River Findhorn

gate c. grid

Allt Fionnach

624m

c. gr. br.

plank brs.

Caimhlin Mor 660m

779m

Continued opposite

Cont'd River Findhorn 3

1 km

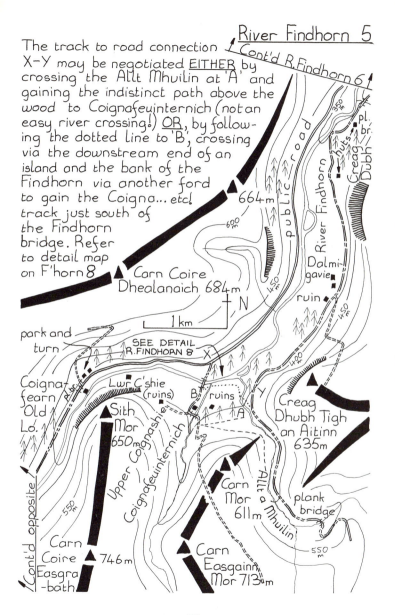

Cont'd R.Findhorn 6

The track to road connection X-Y may be negotiated EITHER by crossing the Allt Mhuilin at 'A' and gaining the indistinct path above the wood to Coignafeuinternich (not an easy river crossing!) OR, by following the dotted line to 'B', crossing via the downstream end of an island and the bank of the Findhorn via another ford to gain the Coigna... etc! track just south of the Findhorn bridge. Refer to detail map on F'horn 8

pl. br.

Creag Dubh

huts

public road

River Findhorn

664m

600 m

Dalmi-gavie

ruin

Carn Coire Dhealanaich 684m

N

1 km

SEE DETAIL R.FINDHORN 8

park and turn

Coigna-fearn Old Lo.

Lwr C'shie (ruins)

B ruins

X

A

Creag Dhubh Tigh an Aitinn 635m

Sith Mor 650m

Upper Coignashie

Coignafeuinternich

Carn Mor 611m

Allt a Mhuilin

plank bridge

550 m

550 m

Cont'd opposite

Carn Coire Easgra-bath

746m

Carn Easgainn Mor 713 m

79

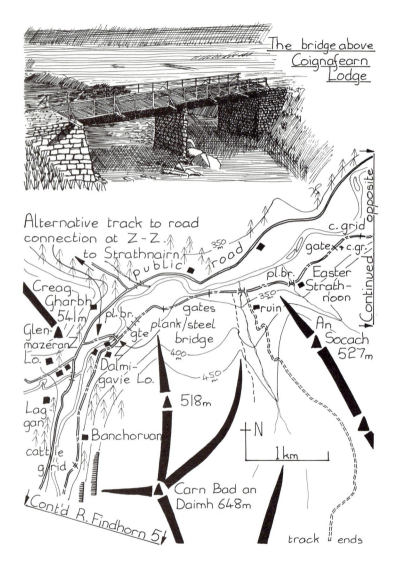

The bridge above Coignafearn Lodge

Alternative track to road connection at Z-Z.

to Strathnairn

Continued opposite

c.grid

gate c.gr.

350 road

public road

pl.br. Easter Strathnoon

350

ruin

Creag Gharbh 541m

pl.br.

gates

plank/steel bridge

An Socach 527m

Glenmazeran Lo.

gte

400 m

450 m

Dalmigavie Lo.

Lag gan

518m

Banchor

cattle grid

N

1 km

Carn Bad an Daimh 648m

Cont'd R. Findhorn 5

track ends

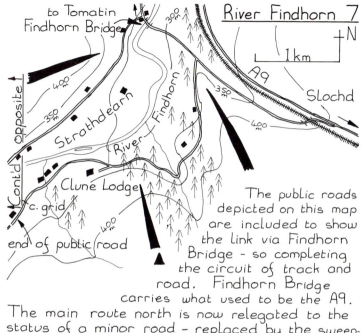

to Tomatin
Findhorn Bridge

+N

1 km

A9

Slochd

400ᵐ

350ᵐ

Strathdearn

River Findhorn

350ᵐ

400ᵐ

Cont'd opposite !

Clune Lodge

c. grid

end of public road

400ᵐ

The public roads
depicted on this map
are included to show
the link via Findhorn
Bridge - so completing
the circuit of track and
road. Findhorn Bridge
carries what used to be the A9.
The main route north is now relegated to the
status of a minor road - replaced by the sweep-
ing curves of the new A9, carrying unseeing
visitors north to Inverness. It is worth taking
time to seek out these bits of old road and to
ponder what life was like just a few years ago
when the railway and the winding 'minor' road
were the only way north. Surely a more civilis-
ed age. Now, speed and cost rule. But what
about our landscape, sliced in half by tarmac,
noise and fumes? No provision is yet made for
the cyclist even using the abandoned road.
Cycleways are an even newer "invention" but we
still have to dice with death on the so-called
"killer" A9, between Tomatin and Slochd. Cyclists
are forgotten in the unrelenting quest for speed
and progress. Stop grousing man and get on
with it! This is supposed to be a guide book!!

81

River Findhorn 8

Mid-Findhorn track-to-road connection - detail map of route X - Y.

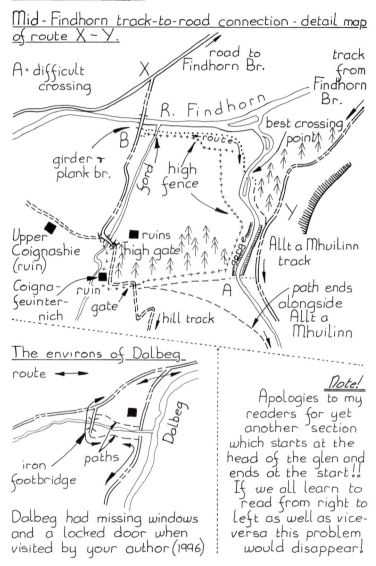

A = difficult crossing

X

road to Findhorn Br.

track from Findhorn Br.

R. Findhorn

B

girder ⊤ plank br.

route

best crossing point

ford

high fence

high gate

ruins

Upper Coignashie (ruin)

Coigna-feuinter-nich

ruin

gate

hill track

A

orange

Allt a Mhuilinn track

path ends alongside Allt a Mhuilinn

The environs of Dalbeg

route ←→

iron footbridge

paths

Dalbeg

Dalbeg had missing windows and a locked door when visited by your author (1996)

Note!
Apologies to my readers for yet another section which starts at the head of the glen and ends at the start!! If we all learn to read from right to left as well as vice-versa this problem would disappear!

82

The Markie Burn provides the Spey dam and the Treig-Laggan hydro scheme with its most easterly source of water, for the Lochaber aluminium works in Fort William. The track also provides the walker with access to an interesting glen surrounded by fine mountains. The number of gates will frustrate cyclists who will have to abandon their mounts at the last gate and continue on foot. The track extends for 5km (3miles), and the path for a further 4km (2.5miles) before petering out above the gorge.

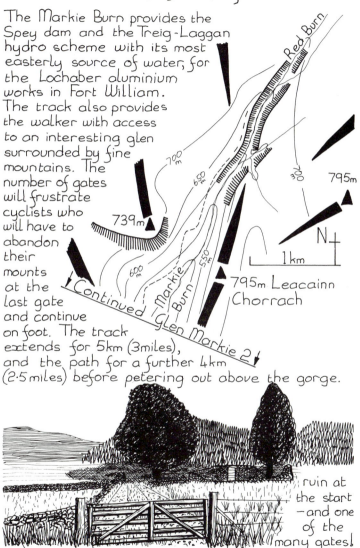

Red Burn

700 m

650 m

700 m

300 m

795m

739m

600 m

550 m

Continued Glen Markie 2

Markie Burn

795m Leacainn Chorrach

N

1 km

ruin at the start —and one of the many gates!

Glen Markie 2 (Spey Dam)

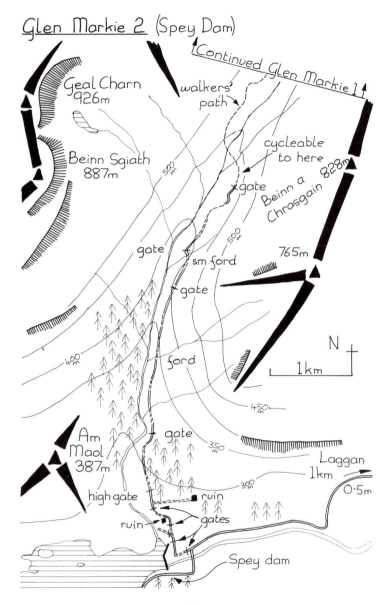

Continued Glen Markie 1

Geal Charn 926m

walkers' path

Beinn Sgiath 887m

cycleable to here

gate

Beinn a Chrasgain 828m

500m

500m

765m

gate

sm.ford

gate

N

1km

ford

450m

Am Maol 387m

gate

350m

Laggan 1km

0.5m

high gate

300m

ruin

gates

ruin

Spey dam

84

The Glen Banchor track extends some 11 km or 7m from Cluny Castle to the minor road north west of Newtonmore, about 3km or 1·5m from the village. The track cuts north of some minor hills and gives access to a branch path (below) and track north to the mountains. Glen Banchor is worth exploring in its own right; on a bike it is best approached from Cluny Castle as the rough section (not really a bike ride!) is tackled downhill. There is a bothy half way which kept your author and his wife dry in a downpour.

The River Calder is not, like your author, an escapee from Yorkshire; I have it on good authority that its namesake still flows through Brighouse, but somehow lacks the sparkle of its northern counterpart!

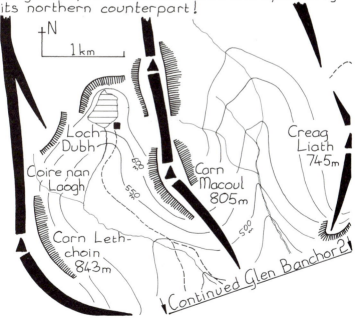

Continued Glen Banchor 2

Glen Banchor 2

Continued Glen Banchor 1

Note the strange course of X the burn An t-Eileach which parts company with Allt Madagain and flows down a different glen.

Continued opposite

Dalballoch (ruin)

Sron na Creige

Allt Madagain

X gates + bothy

450

400

Creag Shiaraidh 559m

N

1 km

An t-Eileach

400

Binnein Mor 550m

Strath an Eilich

350

300

see detail map opposite

A86

250 m to

Cluny Cas.

Newtonmore 8km/5m

The bothy :- The smoke is a result of your author's over optimistic imagination!

86

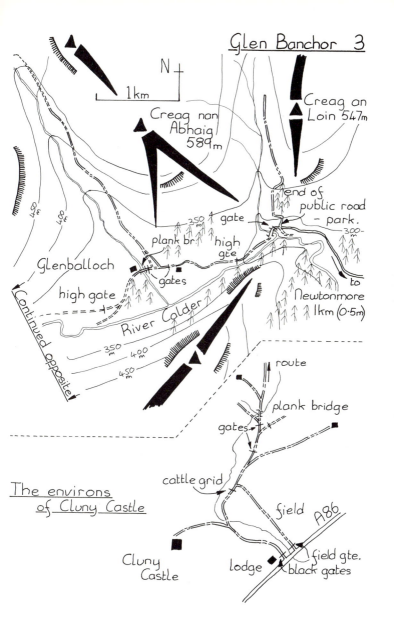

N

1km

Creag nan Abhaig 589m

Creag an Loin 547m

450m

400m

end of public road – park.

300 m

350 m gate

plank br.

high gte

gates

Glenballoch

high gate

River Calder

350 m

400

450 m

to Newtonmore 1km (0.5m)

Continued opposite

route

plank bridge

gates

cattle grid

The environs of Cluny Castle

field

A86

Cluny Castle

lodge

field gte.

black gates

87

Glen Gynack 1

The Glen Gynack track rises first on a public road steeply out of the centre of Kingussie, then levels past the golf course. After Pitmain Lodge it commences a steep climb interrupted only by the crossing of the burn, Allt Mor, before a huge climb to the watershed, and just beyond at over 760m, that's 2500 ft! This route is ideal for anyone with a surplus of energy, climbing 540m (1770 feet) in 8km (5 miles).

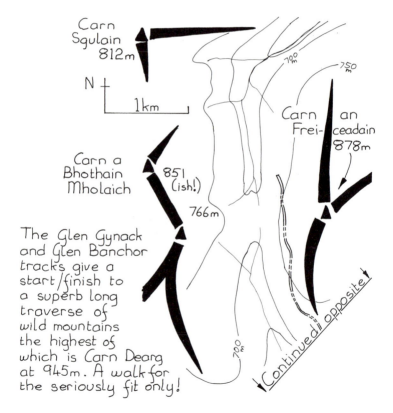

Carn
Squlain
812m

N

1km

Carn an
Frei-ceadain
878m

Carn a
Bhothain
Mholaich

851
(ish!)

766m

The Glen Gynack and Glen Banchor tracks give a start/finish to a superb long traverse of wild mountains the highest of which is Carn Dearg at 945m. A walk for the seriously fit only!

700m

750m

700m

Continued opposite

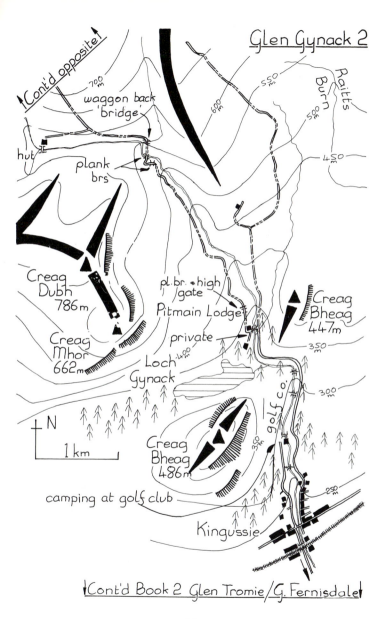

Raitt's Burn

Cont'd opposite

700 m

600 m

550 m

500 m

450 m

waggon back 'bridge'

hut

plank brs

Creag Dubh 786m

Creag Mhor 662m

pl. br. + high gate

Pitmain Lodge

private

Loch Gynack

400 m

Creag Bheag 447m

350 m

300 m

golf co.

N

1 km

Creag Bheag 486m

350 m

250 m

camping at golf club

Kingussie

Cont'd Book 2 Glen Tromie / G. Fernisdale

Raitts Burn 1

Raitts Burn offers a pleasant, if short, sortie through superb mixed woodland leading to open grouse moor. The track ends amid wild country only 7·5 km or about 4·5 miles from the busy A9. The track is only half a mile from the Glen Gynack tracks but to make the connection entails a tramp over rough heather. The Raitts Burn track offers extensive views to the south as height is gained - well worth the effort.

Detail of the start

high gate

Balavil

Fountain-head

old mill

white gates

Mains of Balavil

A9

B9152

care crossing!

Note

the only car parking space is in Kingussie or about a mile N.E. on the B'rd.

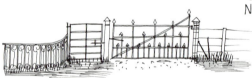

Elaborate gates at the start.

Trees engulf the remains of the old mill

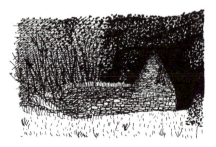

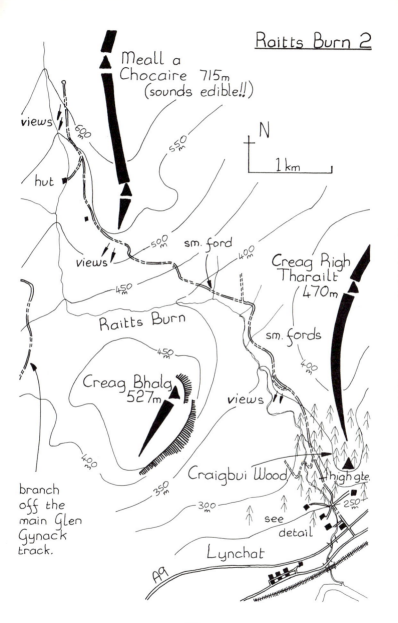

Meall a Chocaire 715m (sounds edible!!)

views

600m

550m

N

1 km

hut

500m

sm. ford

400m

views

450m

Creag Righ Tharailt 470m

Raitts Burn

sm. fords

400m

450m

Creag Bhalg 527m

views

400m

Craigbui Wood

high gte.

350m

branch off the main Glen Gynack track.

300m

see detail

250m

Lynchat

A9

River Dulnain 1

The River Dulnain flows down a very high glen.
No part of this route is below 310m or 1000feet.
This glen may be enjoyed on a bike, on foot and
not infrequently on skis. The upper reaches are
pathless and remote; the only ways out of the
head of the glen are either the long trek to
the Slochd or the hill tracks to Strathspey.
The map below gives distances of this and the
adjacent routes. There is emergency shelter
(just!) at Eil; at Craggan; at the red bothy,
and a further bothy up the Feithlinn. Care is
needed not to underestimate the long distances involved with these routes. The reward
is a superb high glen with an insight into
the tough farm life
that once excisted
(thrived?) in the
glen. The Dulnain
is to be savoured!
Refer to Link
Route 3 at
the end of
this book.

Distances in
km (miles)

92

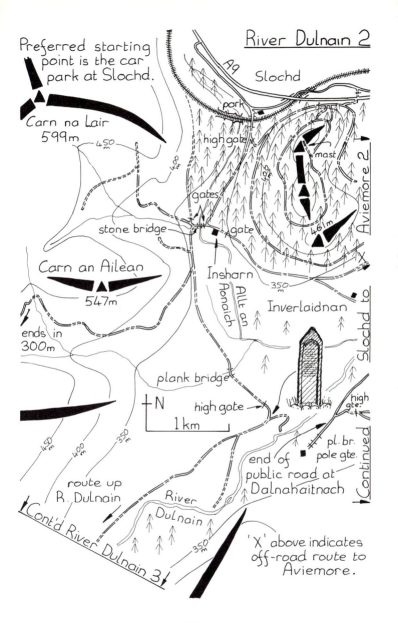

River Dulnain 2

Preferred starting point is the car park at Slochd.

Carn na Lair 599m

Slochd

A9

park

high gate

mast

461m

Aviemore 2

gates

stone bridge

gate

Carn an Ailean 547m

Insharn

Allt an Aonaich

Inverlaidnan

Slochd to

ends in 300m

plank bridge

N
1 km

high gate

high gte.

pl. br. pole gte.

Continued

route up R. Dulnain

River Dulnain

end of public road at Dalnahaitnach

Cont'd River Dulnain 3

'X' above indicates off-road route to Aviemore.

93

River Dulnain 3

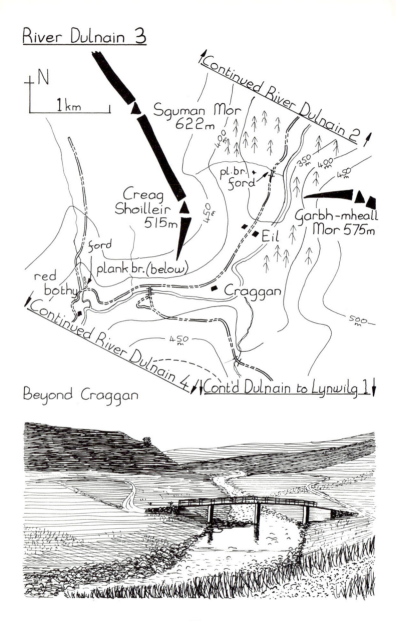

Continued River Dulnain 2

Sguman Mor
622m

pl. br.
ford

Creag
Shoilleir
515m

450m

400m

350m

400m

450m

Garbh-mheall
Mor 575m

Eil

ford

plank br. (below)

red
bothy

Continued River Dulnain 4

Craggan

500m

450m

Cont'd Dulnain to Lynwilg 1

Beyond Craggan

+N

1km

The marked absence of tracks beyond the red bothy makes the upper Dulnain and the links to Alvie and Loch Insh the province of the walker and ski-tourer. Bikes must head for the Spey just after Craggan -to Lynwilg.

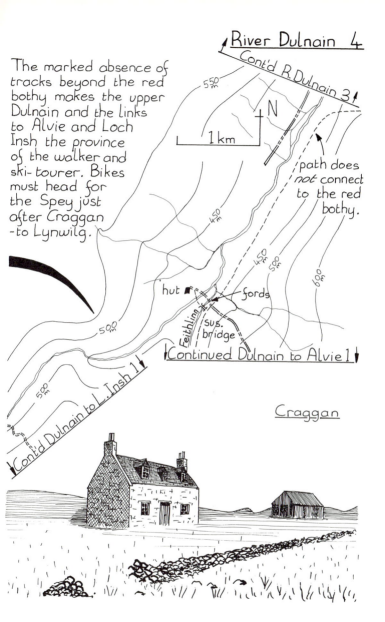

River Dulnain 4

Cont'd R. Dulnain 3

550 m

N

1 km

450 m

path does *not* connect to the red bothy.

450
500
600

hut

fords

Feithlim

sus. bridge

Continued Dulnain to Alvie 1

500 m

500 m

Cont'd Dulnain to L. Insh 1

Craggan

Dulnain to Loch Insh 1

Routes between the Dulnain and Loch Insh, and
Alvie are best combined into a long walk from
Kincraig, or a long through walk from or to the
Slochd. Distances are given on River Dulnain 1.
Cyclists should use the Slochd / Lynwilg tracks
as Alvie Estate do not encourage the use of
bikes on their tracks. In any case, Dulnain - L.
Insh and Dulnain - Alvie are only linked by
a walkers' path. There is shelter at the bothies
-please respect these open shelters.

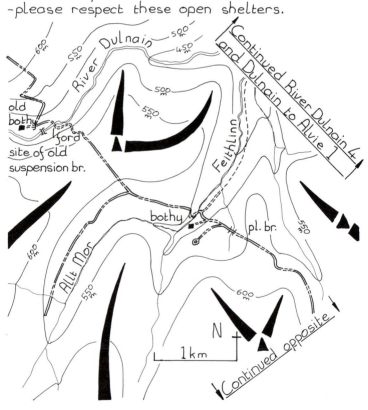

Continued River Dulnain 4 and Dulnain to Alvie 1

Continued opposite

River Dulnain

old bothy

ford

site of old suspension br.

Feithlinn

bothy

pl. br.

Allt Mor

N

1 km

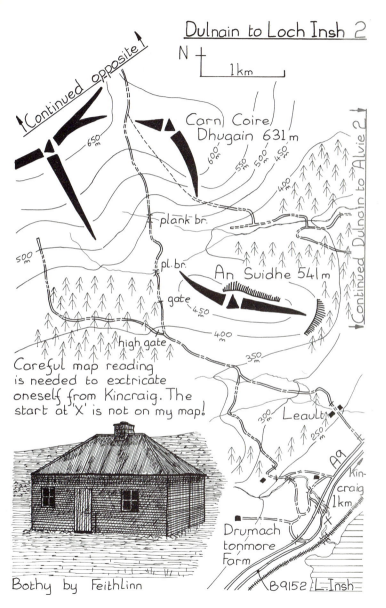

N

1km

Continued opposite

650 m

Carn Coire Dhugain 631m

600 m

550 m

500 m

450 m

400 m

plank br.

500 m

pl. br.

An Suidhe 541m

gate

450

Continued Dulnain to Alvie 2

high gate

400

350

Careful map reading
is needed to extricate
oneself from Kincraig. The
start at 'X' is not on my map!

Leault

300 m

250 m

A9

Kincraig
1km

Drumach
tonmore
Farm

B9152 L.Insh

Bothy by Feithlinn

97

Dulnain to Alvie 1

The middle route of the three passes between the upper River Dulnain and the Spey provides a fine long walk when combined with Dulnain to Loch Insh. (Distance map on R.Dulnain1). I must stress 'walk' as the estate discourage cycling on this and the preceding routes. They are, in any event, linked only by footpath along the Feithlinn, thence by another path via Craggan.

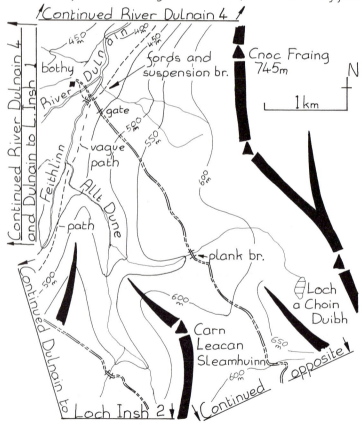

Continued River Dulnain 4

Continued River Dulnain 4 and Dulnain to L.Insh 1

Continued Dulnain to Loch Insh 2

bothy

River Dulnain

fords and suspension br.

Cnoc Fraing 745m

N

1 km

gate

500 m

550 m

vague path

Feithlinn

Allt Dune

600 m

path

500 m

plank br.

600 m

Loch a Choin Duibh

Carn Leacan Sleamhuinn

650 m

600 m

Continued opposite

Loch Insh 2

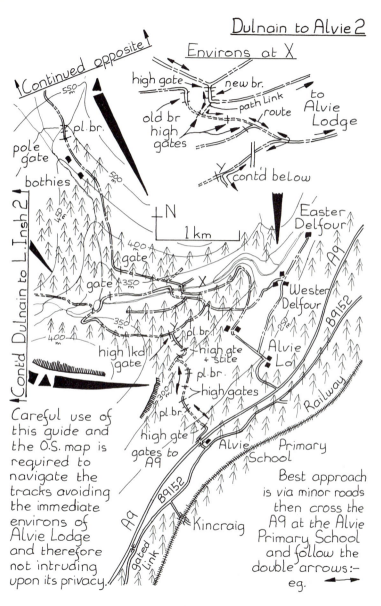

Environs at X

Continued opposite

high gate   new br.
old br   path Link
high   route
gates   to Alvie Lodge

Y contd below

550 m
pl. br.
pole gate
bothies
500

N
1 km

450

400
gate
gate   350

400
350
high lkd gate
X

Easter Delfour
A9

Wester Delfour
250 m

pl. br.
high ate + stile
pl. br.
high gates
pl. br.
high gte
gates to A9

Alvie Lo

Railway
B9152

Alvie Primary School

Contd Dulnain to L.Insh 2

Careful use of this guide and the O.S. map is required to navigate the tracks avoiding the immediate environs of Alvie Lodge and therefore not intruding upon its privacy.

A9   B9152   Kincraig
gated Link

Best approach is via minor roads then cross the A9 at the Alvie Primary School and follow the double arrows:-
eg. ⬌

↑Continued River Dulnain 3 ↑

Large plank bridge 400m

•• Craggan

R. Dulnain

500m

1km

N

←Cont'd R. Dulnain 4

450m

400m

plank bridge

500m

Allt Ghuithais

Geal-charn Beag 741m

600m

An excellent track rises from the Dulnain to pass over the col at a height of 690m before revealing the finest views of the Cairngorms from the north west. The true scale of these mountains can be appreciated from a viewpoint half their altitude, and they appear far grander than when seen from Aviemore. The steep track is superb - fine for either an out-and-back sortie from Aviemore or an extended trip from the Slochd. Either way, make sure a clear day is chosen for the views!

650m

cairns

700m

Geal-charn Mor 824m

Continued opposite→

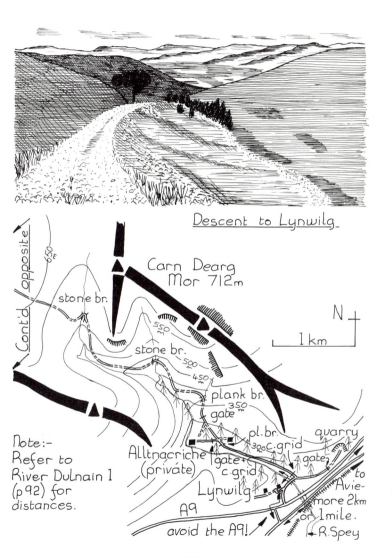

Descent to Lynwilg

Carn Dearg
Mor 712m

stone br.

550m

stone br.

500m

450m

plank br.

350m

gate

pl.br.

quarry

300 c.grid

Alltnacriche gate

(priváte)

c.grid

Lynwilg

gate

to Aviemore 2km or 1mile.

A9

avoid the A9!

R.Spey

N

1 km

Cont'd opposite

650m

Note:-
Refer to
River Dulnain 1
(p 92) for
distances.

Slochd to Aviemore 1

The off-road route from Slochd to Aviemore is both complex and rewarding. It explores the ancient Sluggan Bridge (superior in your author's opinion to the old bridge at Carrbridge), and a good length of General Wade's Military Road. (Where would mountainbikers be without General Wade?) The route then follows forest tracks south to Aviemore - almost. There are several connections to the road giving access to Carrbridge, Boat of Garten and the surrounding public roads, making Slochd/Dulnain/Lynwilg/Aviemore/Slochd per Link Route 3 possible from several start/finish points. The total distance from Slochd to Aviemore is about 18km or 11·5 miles. There is no shelter other than a quick exit to a cafe in Carrbridge or Boat. Details of the many road connections are given on Slochd to Aviemore 4. The route is generally slow going on a bike with a lot of map reading and some rough sections. Beware of the ford on G.W.M.R. (top of page 104); this can become a paddle in wet weather.

The bridge at Insharn

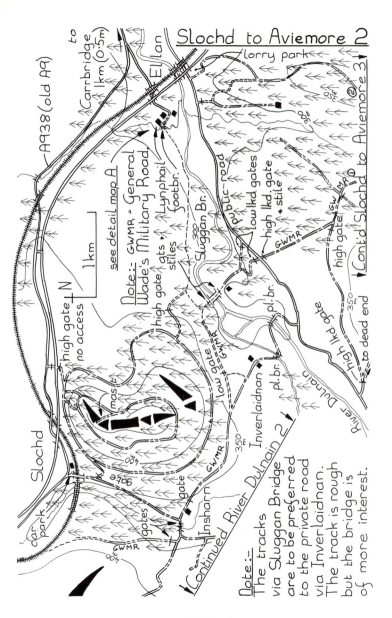

Slochd to Aviemore 2

to Carrbridge 1km (0.5m)

A938 (old A9)

Carrbridge 1km

to lorry park

Ellan

see detail map A

Note:- GWMR = General Wade's Military Road

Lynphail footbr.

Lynphail stiles

gts

high gate

Sluggan Br.

public road

low lkd gates

high lkd. gate stile

GWMR

high gate

GW MR

@ 350

300

30c

Cont'd Slochd to Aviemore 3

high gate N no access

1 km

pl.br.

350

high lkd gate

to dead end

Slochd

mast

GWMR

low gate

River Dulnain

car park

400

gate

350

GWMR

Insharn

Inverlaidnan 2

pl.br.

gates

GWMR

450

Continued River Dulnain 2

Note:-
The tracks via Sluggan Bridge are to be preferred to the private road via Inverlaidnan. The track is rough but the bridge is of more interest.

103

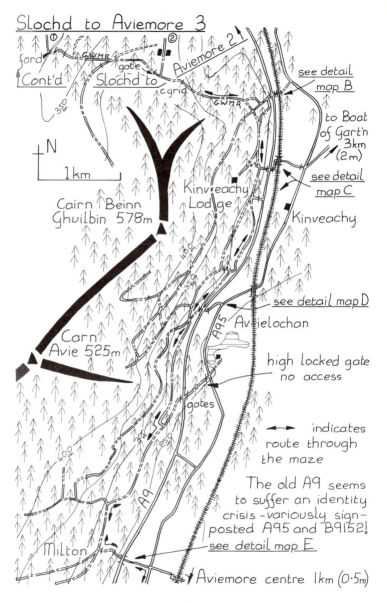

ford
Cont'd

GWMR

gate

Slochd to

Aviemore 2

c.grid

GWMR

350

N

1 km

see detail
map B

to Boat
of Gart'n
3 km
(2 m)

see detail
map C

Kinveachy
Lodge

Cairn Beinn
Ghuilbin 578m

Kinveachy

400 m

350 m

Carn
Avie 525m

see detail map D

A95

Avielochan

high locked gate
no access

gates

250 m

250 m

◄──► indicates
route through
the maze

400 m

A9

The old A9 seems
to suffer an identity
crisis - variously sign-
posted A95 and B9152!

see detail map E

Milton

Aviemore centre 1km (0·5m)

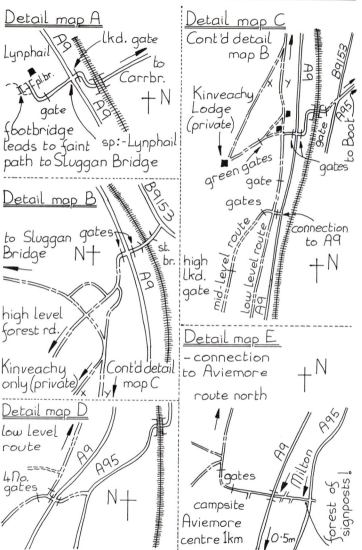

Detail map A

Lynphail

A9

lkd. gate

to Carrbr.

F.pl.br.

gate

+ N

footbridge leads to faint path to Sluggan Bridge

sp:-Lynphail

A9

Detail map B

B9153

to Sluggan Bridge

N+

gates

st. br.

A9

high level forest rd.

Kinveachy only (private)

x

y

Cont'd detail map C

Detail map C

Cont'd detail map B

Kinveachy Lodge (private)

A9

B9153

x

y

A95

gate

gates

to Boat

green gates

gate

gates

high lkd. gate

mid-level route

low level route

connection to A9

+ N

A9

Detail map D

low level route

4No. gates

A9

A95

N+

Detail map E

– connection to Aviemore route north

+ N

A9

A95

Milton

gates

campsite

Aviemore centre 1km

0.5m

forest of signposts!

Moray

Moray

Access:- East of the A9 and south of the Moray Firth, bounded by the roads through Elgin, Charlestown of Aberlour and Grantown on Spey, this region offers some good walking and off road cycling. This is based on forest, glen and, at Dava, an old railway line. It is indeed a pity that some estates in the region discourage access to forest and moor. If the Forestry Commission can successfully combine conservation and commercial forestry with public access as at Culbin Forest, your simple-minded author fails to appreciate the problem of public access (and bike access) elsewhere; apart from grouse moor during the shooting season of course. Indeed - one of the areas where bike access is forbidden is so good for off-road cycling there would be scope for the estate to derive an income from the activity! Is anyone out there listening!!!?

Accommodation:- Mainly in the centres of Grantown, Inverness and Nairn, which, together with Carrbridge, Forres and Elgin have Tourist Information Centres. Only Inverness and Elgin are open all year. There are very busy Youth Hostels in Inverness, and Aviemore which is too far south for Moray. The few camp sites are scattered around the edges of the region.

Geographical Features:- A gently undulating area rising to high moorland in the south before dropping down into Strathspey. (NOT the "Spey Valley" *please!!*) Why Anglicise a superb Scottish name? I digress! The low hills do, however, provide dramatic *views* - from Morven (Helmsdale) in the north, to Cairngorm in the south. Much of the high ground is grouse moor so watch those dates. I bet the grouse don't look forward to the 'glorious twelfth'!

Rivers:- The region is crossed by several major rivers, from north to south:- the River Nairn, River Findhorn and River Spey, all of which rise deep in the Monadhliath Mountains. The Spey, famous for its salmon, is one of Scotland's finest rivers yet the less well known Findhorn probably passes through better scenery, throughout its turbulent course. The region's only 'home grown' river of any significance is the River Lossie.

Forests:- The major forests are Culbin Forest and Heldon Wood. The area has many smaller woodlands which do not provide worthwhile routes due to their small size. Access is regrettably not encouraged to the best natural woodland around Darnaway and the lower Findhorn although a few forest walks of limited length are laid out.

Lochs:- The most significant loch is Lochindorb, a few miles south west of Dava, but even this shallow pool is only 3km or about 2 miles long. This is drained by the Dorback Burn which joins forces with the River Divie before adding significantly to the Findhorn at Randolph's Leap. Several minor lochans, some little more than puddles, are scattered thinly over the area.

Emergency:- The routes in this region are fairly tame and common sense will keep my reader out of difficulty. The moor track above Dava is exposed at nearly 400m or about 1300ft, and the Glen Lossie and Riereach Burn tracks are a touch over 300m (1000ft). A wary eye should be kept on the weather on these routes but one is always within 4 or 5 miles of civilisation. Go west for the long remote glens of the Monadhliath.

Moray Routes 1

Riereach Burn

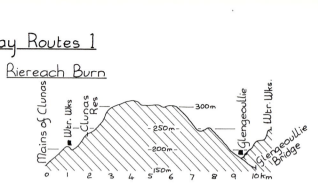

Culbin Forest

Endless tracks between 0m and only 20m

Dava

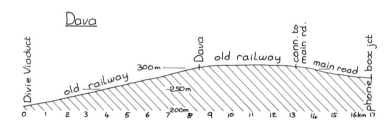

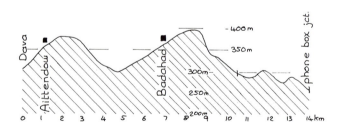

Moray Routes 2

Glen Lossie

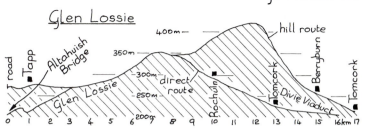

Burn of Rothes

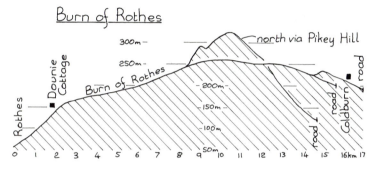

Heldon Wood

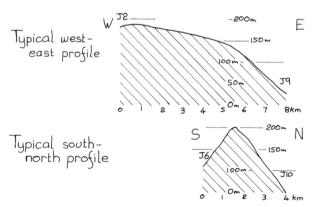

Typical west-east profile

Typical south-north profile

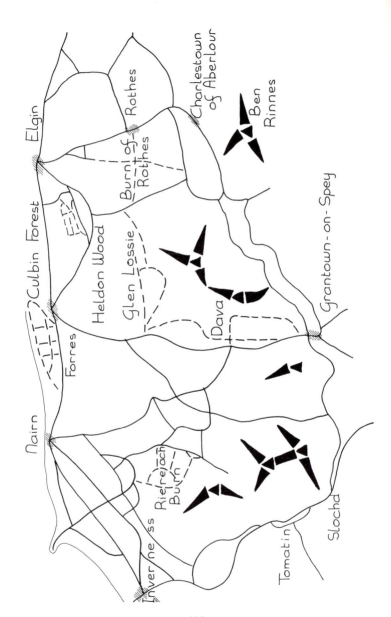

The tracks around Riereach Burn are best approached from the car park at Clunas Reservoir or via the road connection at Glengeoullie. The short 9km (6mile) circuit taking in (almost) the summit of Carn Maol and the ravine of the burn is best completed clockwise to take advantage of the views north. Beware of the rifle range in Achneim Wood. The usual red flag is displayed at the road end of the range. The eastern connection to the public road via Cose is intrusive and best avoided. The rough tracks continue south almost to the Findhorn, forming a longer circuit returning via the road. This is grouse moor - to be avoided during the grouse shooting season. There is no shelter.

The environs of Glengeoullie :-

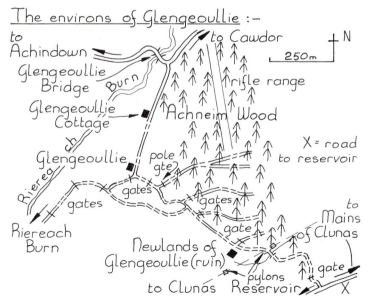

113

Riereach Burn 2

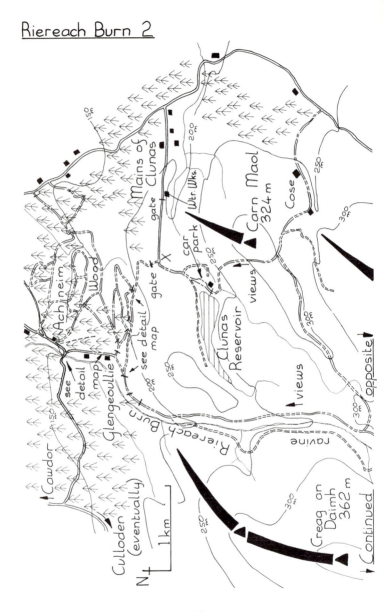

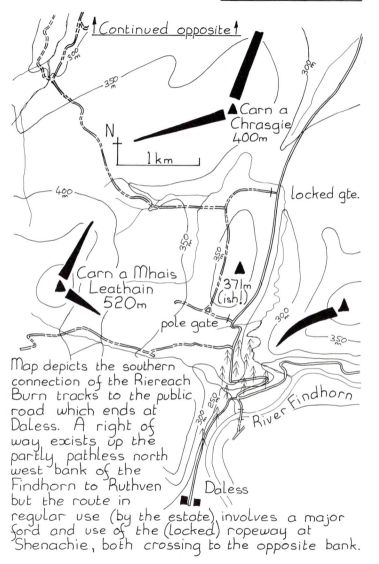

↑ Continued opposite ↑

▲ Carn a Chrasgie 400m

locked gte.

Carn a Mhais Leathain 520m

▲ 371m (ish!)

pole gate

River Findhorn

Daless

Map depicts the southern connection of the Riereach Burn tracks to the public road which ends at Daless. A right of way exists up the partly pathless north west bank of the Findhorn to Ruthven but the route in regular use (by the estate) involves a major ford and use of the (locked) ropeway at Shenachie, both crossing to the opposite bank.

115

Culbin Forest 1

Culbin Forest comprises an area some 14km by 4km (9 x 2½ miles) interlaced with mainly level tracks. It is an area of exceptional interest being one of the most important areas of dunes in Europe. The forest is an S.S.S.I. and Forest Enterprise produce a very informative leaflet detailing the unique geomorphology. The forest was planted to stabilize the shifting dunes, which have moved the Findhorn estuary some miles to the east and reputedly claimed farms. The old estuary continues to fill with silt as a study of old maps reveals.... Most of the track junctions are numbered - to make getting lost more difficult — although one can become completely lost and just refer to the numbers to re-locate! At least two days on a bike are needed to fully explore the forest. Coast or public road are never far away. Best starting points are Cloddymoss car park or the picnic area at Wellhill.

The Bar (sadly only serves sand!!)

views

21

Y

Z

22

24

23

Loch Loy

L. Loy

Continued opposite

public road

pole gates

high locked gate

+ high stile (no bikes)

to Nairn

locked gate

Culbin Forest is a shining example of how commercial forestry, conservation and leisure activities can happily co-exist. Walking, mountainbiking, horse-riding, ornithology, geology, geomorphology, and many more "ologies"! Private landowners often restrict access on conservation or safety grounds... (cont'd below)

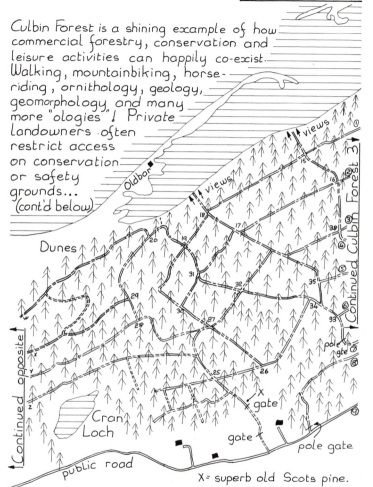

Oldbar

views

views

views

Dunes

Continued opposite

Continued Culbin Forest 3

pole gate

gate

X gate

Cran Loch

gate

pole gate

public road

X = superb old Scots pine.

- these excuses are brought into sharp focus when set against Culbin Forest. Let's at least have authentic reasons for any access restriction then an honest discussion may just be possible.

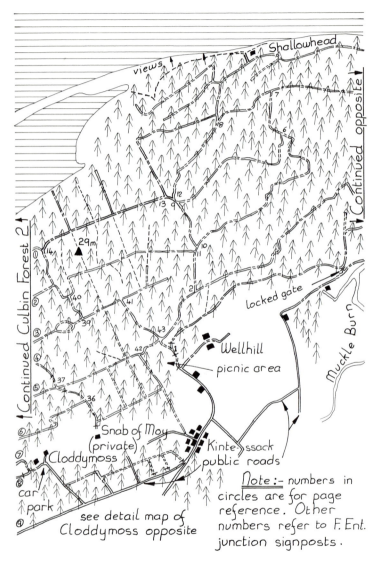

Shallowhead

views

Continued opposite

Continued Culbin Forest 2

29m

locked gate

Muckle Burn

Wellhill

picnic area

Snab of Moy
(private)

Cloddymoss

Kinte-ssack
public roads

car
park

see detail map of
Cloddymoss opposite

<u>Note</u>:- numbers in
circles are for page
reference. Other
numbers refer to F. Ent.
junction signposts.

118

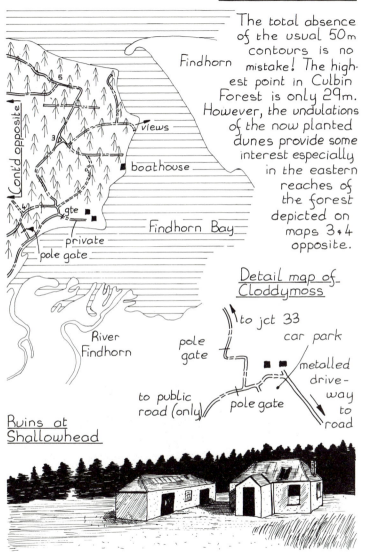

The total absence of the usual 50m contours is no mistake! The highest point in Culbin Forest is only 29m. However, the undulations of the now planted dunes provide some interest especially in the eastern reaches of the forest depicted on maps 3 & 4 opposite.

Findhorn

Findhorn Bay

views

boathouse

gte

private

pole gate

River Findhorn

Detail map of Cloddymoss

to jct 33

car park

pole gate

metalled drive-way to road

to public road (only)

pole gate

Ruins at Shallowhead

Dava 1

The tracks centred on Dava comprise a length of disused railway line rideable for some 12km ('8miles), running north and south of Dava. To the east a moor track runs for some 4km before cutting <u>south</u> past Huntly's Cave to Auchnagallin. The public roads have to be used to link moor track to railway at the southern end (this includes a couple of miles of 'A' road). Similarly, a short section of road has to be used immediately <u>north</u> of Dava to avoid houses, the old station etc. The railway can be followed to the viaduct at Glenernie. Refer to link route 4 as Dava is directly connected to Glen Lossie and in turn to Burn of Rothes. There is emergency shelter 1km north of the ruin at Bodahad. Treat with respect please - this is private! Distances are detailed below:-

<u>Note:-</u> The old railway line has the addition of 'sleepers' ie:- ⧾⧾⧾ superimposed on the usual graded track symbols.

120

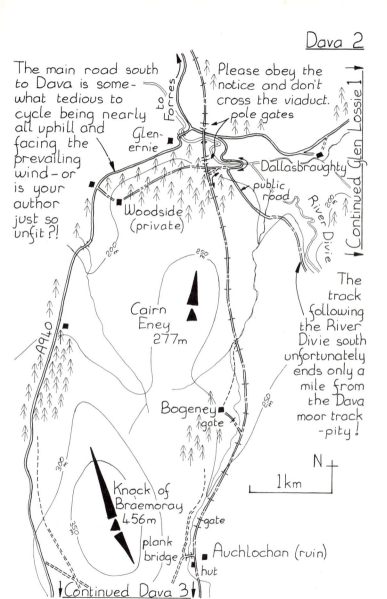

The main road south to Dava is somewhat tedious to cycle being nearly all uphill and facing the prevailing wind – or is your author just so unfit?!

Please obey the notice and don't cross the viaduct. pole gates

to Forres

Glenernie

Woodside (private)

Dallasbraughty

public road

River Divie

Continued Glen Lossie 1

The track following the River Divie south unfortunately ends only a mile from the Dava moor track – pity!

200 m

250 m

Cairn Eney 277m

A940

Bogeney gate

250 m

N

1 km

300 m

350

Knock of Braemoray 456m

plank bridge

gate

Auchlochan (ruin)

hut

Continued Dava 3

Dava 3

↑Continued Dava 2↑

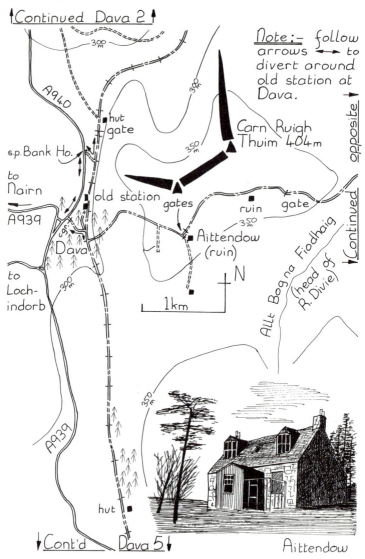

300m

A940

hut
gate

s.p. Bank Ho.

to
Nairn

A939

old station

Dava

gates

350m

350m

Carn Ruigh
Thuim 404m

Note:- follow arrows ⟷ to divert around old station at Dava.

opposite →

← Continued →

ruin

gate

Aittendow
(ruin)

350m

Allt Bogna Fiodhaig
(head of
R. Divie)

to
Loch-
indorb

300m

N

1km

350m

↓Cont'd↓ Dava 5↓

hut

Aittendow

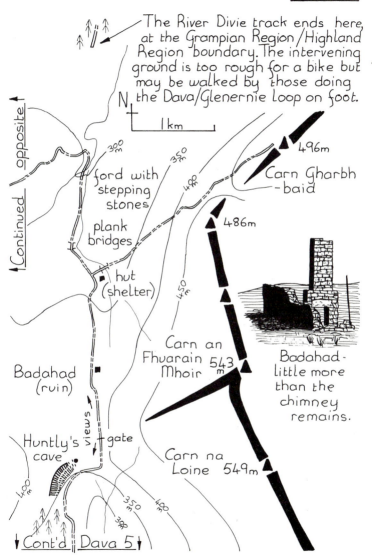

The River Divie track ends here, at the Grampian Region/Highland Region boundary. The intervening ground is too rough for a bike but may be walked by those doing the Dava/Glenernie loop on foot.

N

1 km

Continued opposite ▶

300m

350

400

ford with stepping stones

plank bridges

hut (shelter)

496m

Carn Gharbh -baid

486m

450

Carn an Fhuarain Mhoir 543 m

Badahad - little more than the chimney remains.

Badahad (ruin)

Huntly's cave

views

gate

Carn na Loine 549m

400m

350 m

400

300

▼ Cont'd ▮ Dava 5 ▼

Dava 5

↑Continued Dava 3↑   ↑Continued Dava 4↑

N

1 km

quarry

parking

gate

gate

locked gate

better conn-
ection to
main road

Upper Derraid

Auchna-
gallin

—— 300

gate

possible connection
to main road

overgrown

As access
to the rail-
way is not
possible via
Upper Derraid
or the bridge X,
the main road
has to be followed
via the 'phone box
to point Y or Z.

350

300

X

phone
box

to Forres

gate

to Divie viaduct

s.p.
'Bank House'

fence-no
way through

old
station

to Nairn

route =

track to
Aitten

c.grid

The environs of Dava

to Grantown

124

The Glen Lossie tracks provide a link between the Forres/Grantown road (and Dava) and the Burn of Rothes tracks - see Link Route 4. The circuit at the western end is best done clockwise to cover the roughest....

Tomnamoon

gate

public road

to Forres

$\frac{200}{m}$ minor

$\frac{250}{m}$

N

1km

gate

old railway

$\frac{300}{m}$

①

Hill of Glaschyle

$\frac{250}{m}$

Johnstripe

gate

$\frac{230}{m}$

gate

②

Divie viaduct

gate

Tomcork

plank br.

gates

Dallasbraughty

Lurg

River Divie

$\frac{200}{m}$

③

Continued Glen Lossie 2

Continued Dava 2

..section downhill. The link between this circuit and G. Lossie 'proper' is not shown on current (1996) O.S. maps. In short, the tracks comprise a circuit from Divie viaduct, a connection north (above) to the minor road, and Glen Lossie to the east, this dividing via Tapp and Aultahuish.

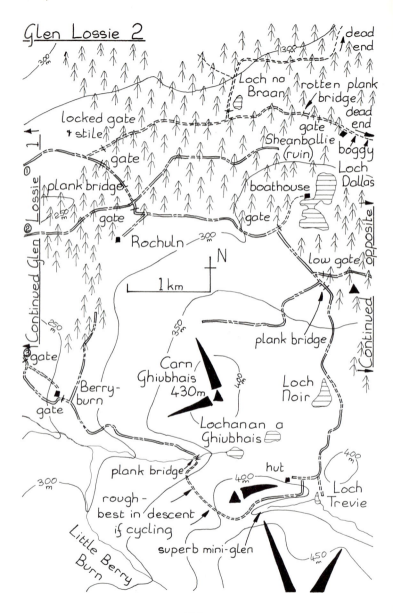

Glen Lossie 2

dead end

300

Loch na Braan

rotten plank bridge

dead end

locked gate + stile

gate

Sheanballie (ruin)

gate

boggy

Loch Dallas

plank bridge

250

gate

boathouse

gate

Continued Glen Lossie

Rochuln

300

low gate

opposite

Continued

250

N

1 km

plank bridge

gate

Berry-burn

gate

350

Carn Ghiubhais 430m

400

Loch Noir

Lochanan a Ghiubhais

plank bridge

rough - best in descent if cycling

400

hut

superb mini-glen

400

Loch Trevie

450

Little Berry Burn

300

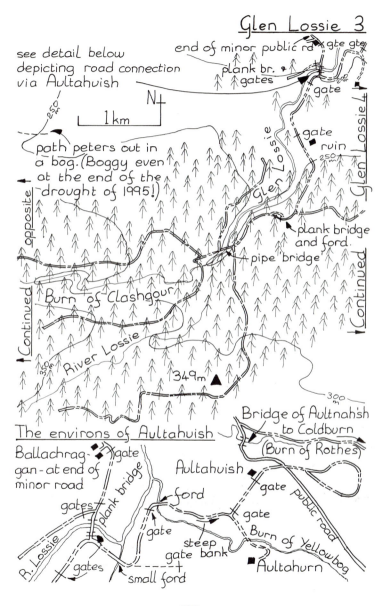

see detail below
depicting road connection
via Aultahuish

end of minor public rd
plank br.
gates
gate
gate
ruin

Glen Lossie 4

path peters out in
a bog. (Boggy even
at the end of the
drought of 1995!)

N

1 km

250m

Continued (opposite)

Glen Lossie

plank bridge
and ford.
pipe bridge

Continued

Burn of Clashgour

River Lossie

349m

300m

The environs of Aultahuish

Ballachrag-
gan - at end of
minor road

gate

gates

plank bridge

R. Lossie

gates

small ford

ford

gate

gate

steep
gate bank

Bridge of Aultnah'sh
to Coldburn
(Burn of Rothes)

Aultahuish

gate

public road

gate

Burn of Yellowbog

Aultahurn

127

Glen Lossie 4

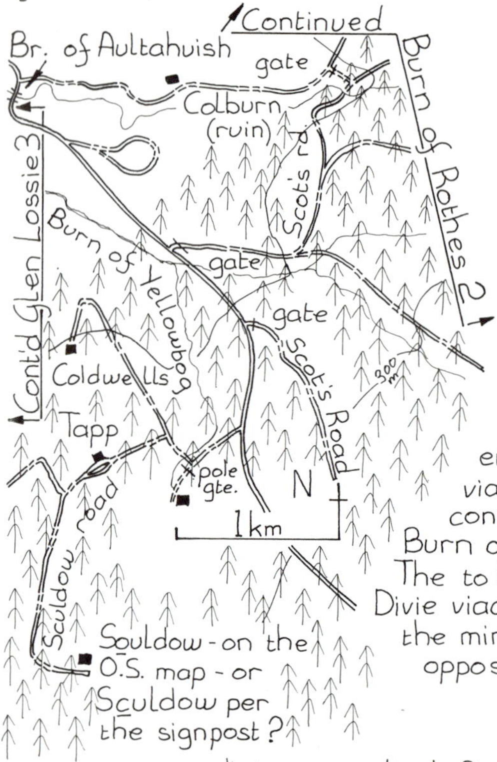

Continued

Br. of Aultahuish
gate
Colburn (ruin)
Burn of Rothes 2
Scot's rd.
Contd Glen Lossie 3
Burn of Yellowbog
gate
gate
Scot's Road
Coldwells
Tapp
pole gte.
N
1 km
Souldow - on the O.S. map - or Sculdow per the signpost?
Sculdow road

This map depicts the eastern end of the Glen Lossie tracks. Refer to the detail map at the foot of the previous page for the route from forest to public road via Aultahuish. An easier track enters the forest via Tapp, and both connect with the Burn of Rothes tracks. The total distance from Divie viaduct (one way) to the minor road shown opposite is 16 km or 10 miles.

Loch Dallas boathouse

The Burn of Rothes tracks extend from Aultahuish Bridge (opposite, Glen Lossie) to Rothes and may be approached either as a 'circular' from Rothes, exploring the eastern end only, or using one of the two tracks north and returning by the road; or alternatively an extended tour incorporating Glen Lossie and the Dava tracks (see Link Route 4). For walkers the circular from Rothes is more appropriate at 14 km or 9 miles. Other distances are given at the foot of this page. There is no shelter.

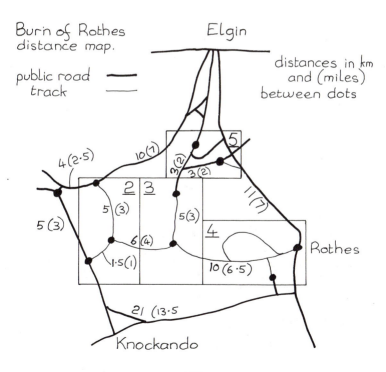

Burn of Rothes distance map.

public road ▬▬
track ▬▬

distances in km and (miles) between dots

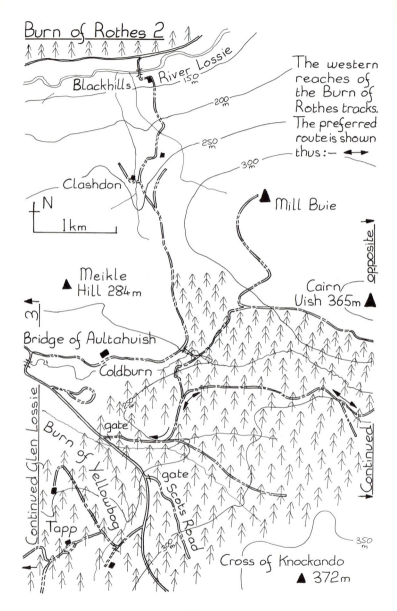

Burn of Rothes 2

The western reaches of the Burn of Rothes tracks. The preferred route is shown thus :— ◄—►

River Lossie

Blackhills

150 m

200 m

250 m

300 m

Clashdon

N
1 km

Mill Buie

Meikle Hill 284 m

Cairn Uish 365 m

opposite ►

Bridge of Aultahuish

Coldburn

◄ 3

gate

Glen Lossie

Burn of Yellowbog

gate

Scots Road

Continued

Continued

Tapp

300 m

350 m

Cross of Knockando
▲ 372 m

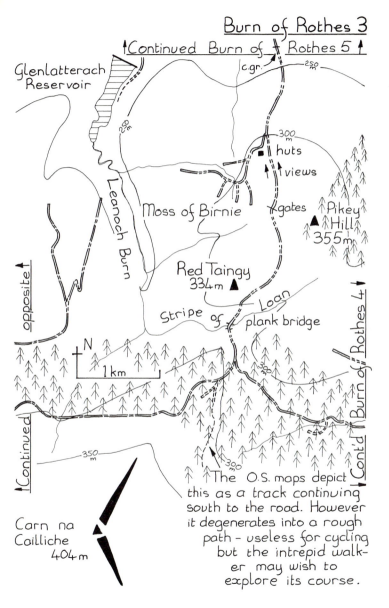

↑<u>Continued Burn of ‡ Rothes 5</u> ↑

c.gr.

250 m

Glenlatterach
Reservoir

250 m

huts

300 m

↑ ↑ views

Moss of Birnie

‡ gates

Leanoch Burn

Red Taingy
334m ▲

Pikey
Hill
355m

↑ <u>opposite</u>

Stripe of ‡ Loan

plank bridge

← <u>Burn of Rothes 4</u> ↑

↑ N

|— 1 km —|

300 m

<u>Cont'd Burn of Rothes 4</u> ↑

↑ <u>Continued</u>

350 m

Carn na
Cailliche
404m

300 m

The O.S. maps depict
this as a track continuing
south to the road. However
it degenerates into a rough
path – useless for cycling
but the intrepid walk-
er may wish to
explore its course.

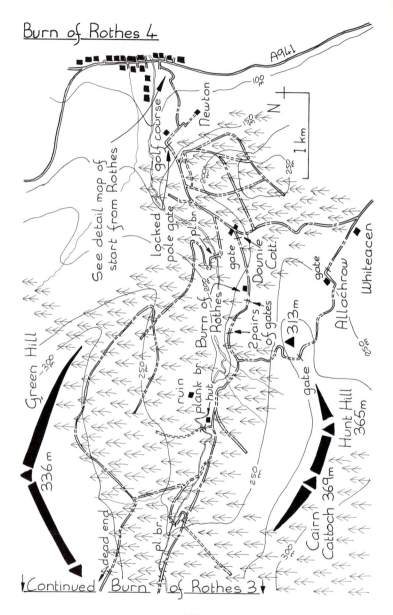

A941

100 m

Newton

150 m

250 m

N

1 km

golf course

See detail map of start from Rothes

locked pole gate

pl. br.

gate

200 m

Dounie Cott.

Whiteacen

gate

Allachrow

250 m

Burn of Rothes

2 pairs of gates

▲ 313 m

Green Hill

300 m

250 m

ruin

plank br.
hut

gate

gate

Hunt Hill 365 m

▲ 336 m

▲ Cairn Cattoch 369 m

250 m

200 m

dead end

pl. br.

↓ Continued Burn of Rothes 3 ↓

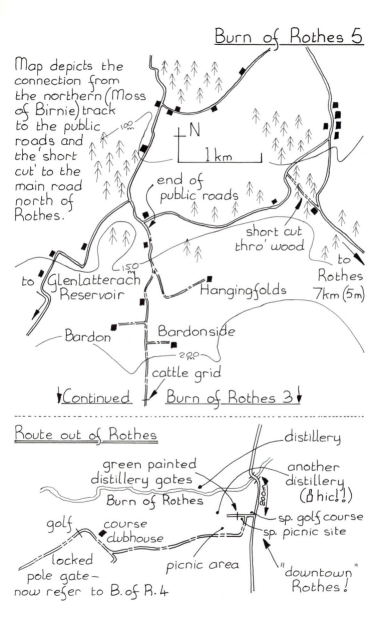

Map depicts the connection from the northern (Moss of Birnie) track to the public roads and the 'short cut' to the main road north of Rothes.

N

1 km

100 m

end of public roads

short cut thro' wood

to Rothes 7km (5m)

150 m

to Glenlatterach Reservoir

Hangingfolds

Bardon

Bardonside

200 m

cattle grid

↓Continued ↓ Burn of Rothes 3↓

Route out of Rothes

distillery

green painted distillery gates

another distillery (☺ hic!!)

Burn of Rothes

200 m

golf course clubhouse

sp. golf course

sp. picnic site

picnic area

locked pole gate — now refer to B. of R. 4

"downtown" Rothes!

Heldon Wood 1

A casual glance at the map would probably lead one to dismiss Heldon Wood (and Monaughty Wood) as covering too small an area to provide sufficient interest. However about 35 miles of forest tracks from "motorway" to footpath, and all grades between, cross and re-cross the forest allowing either the most leisurely stroll or a full day's cycling to be equally enjoyable. There is also a reasonable variety of trees and recent (1996) felling has opened up good views both north and south of the ridge, near to the southern edge of the forest. The wood is, for cyclists, conveniently encircled by minor roads which are included on the maps opposite. Road junctions with forest tracks are numbered J1 to J10 for reference, (not to be confused with page-edge ref. Nos. circled). Cyclists note that the car park has only footpath links (with steps) to the tracks and these should be avoided by cycling 500m along the minor road to J7. Parking is possible at some other junctions as shown :- eg :- J2(p).

N

1 km

J1 pole gate

pole gate

J2(p)

J3(p)
pole gates
J4(p)

J5

Continued opposite

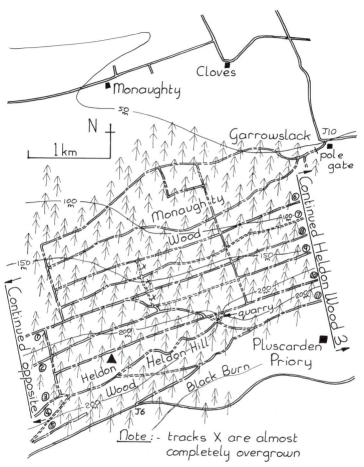

Note :- tracks X are almost completely overgrown

Forest Enterprise sensibly discourage cyclists from using the marked walking trails where these are only footpath width, and have no objection to shared use of the tracks provided cyclists keep their speed down..... fair enough.

Heldon Wood 3

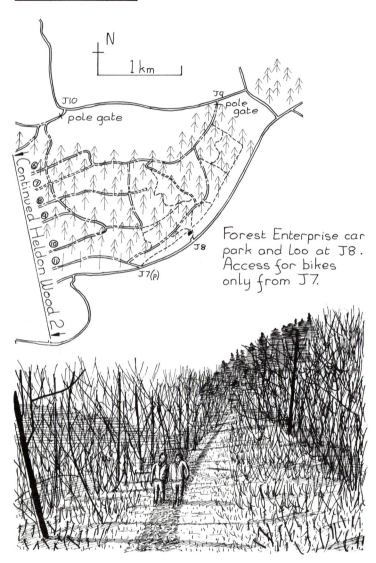

N

1 km

J10
pole gate

J9
pole gate

Continued Heldon Wood 2

⑦
⑧
⑨
⑩
⑪

J8

J7(p)

Forest Enterprise car
park and loo at J8.
Access for bikes
only from J7.

Link Routes

The link routes shown demonstrate how long through routes are made up from the various page maps. Variations can be planned using further adjacent routes but these should provide a basis for extended exploration.

The Great Glen

Link Route 1

An excellent through mountain bike route or long distance walk but NOT an alternative to the road for the touring cyclist on a road bike.

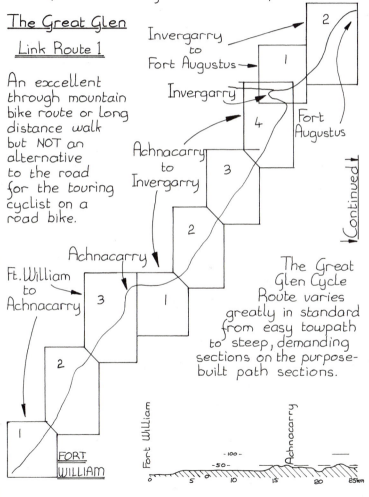

Invergarry to Fort Augustus

Invergarry

Fort Augustus

Achnacarry to Invergarry

Ft. William to Achnacarry

Achnacarry

Continued →

The Great Glen Cycle Route varies greatly in standard from easy towpath to steep, demanding sections on the purpose-built path sections.

FORT WILLIAM

Fort William

Achnacarry

- 100 -
- 50 -

0   5   10   15   20   25km

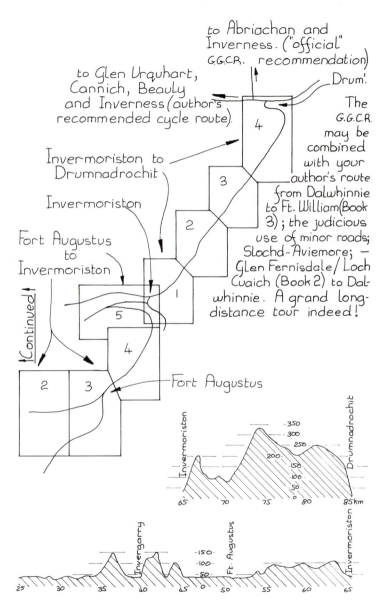

The Corrieyairack, Laggan, and Glen Roy.

This route is a __walk__ for the reasons explained on the detail maps on South Laggan Forest and Glen Gloy though the Corrieyairack Pass may be ridden.

The walk is an exploration of transport history, covering General Wade's roads, ancient paths and the old railway line to Fort Augustus.

The River Dulnain and Aviemore

Link Route 3

An excellent mountainbiking circuit from either Slochd or Aviemore (or Boat of Garten/Carrbridge) giving a ride of approximately 43km or 27miles. A hard day out but extremely rewarding due to the magnificent view of the Cairngorms (ski-ing scars excepted) from the hill above Lynwilg. Please note that the Dulnain/Loch Insh and Dulnain/Alvie routes are for walkers only as they are not connected other than by a faint path to the main Dulnain track.
The Aviemore to Slochd section can be covered on relatively quiet secondary roads if joining or leaving the route at Boat or Carrbridge, but try to include a visit to Sluggan Bridge and please don't cycle on the A9!

Slochd

Slochd-Amore 2

River Dulnain 2

River Dulnain 3

Slochd-Aviemore 3

Dulnain-Lynwilg 1

Dulnain-Lynwilg 2

Aviemore

140

Link Route 4

Three separate routes which, by happy coincidence link together with only a short length of minor road between each. Further, a pleasant quiet 'B' road alongside the picturesque River Findhorn completes a long circuit of some 90km or 56miles. Dava to Rothes is half that at 45km and Grantown to Rothes (by the tracks) is 65km or 40miles.

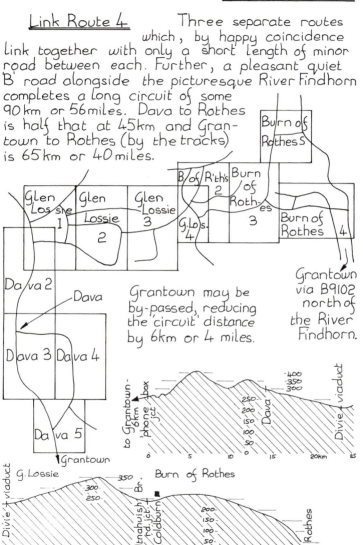

Grantown may be by-passed, reducing the 'circuit' distance by 6km or 4 miles.

Grantown via B9102 north of the River Findhorn.

Glen Markie and the River Findhorn

Link Route 5

A 40km/25m route linking Tomatin to (eventually) Fort Augustus. The higher section, approximately the last 2km of the Findhorn and 6km of upper Glen Markie is a walk, not a bike ride. However 25 miles is a long walk and unless transport is arranged at Killin, there is an additional long road walk to Whitebridge. The bothy is not much use due to its condition. If a bike is taken (carried, dragged, pushed, but not ridden) over the watershed, start from Tomatin, then some of upper Glen Markie may be rideable downhill and in dry conditions. Allow plenty of time and watch the weather, there is no way out other than turning back.

River Findhorn 6

R. F. 7

River Find/horn 5

River Find/horn 4

River Findhorn 2

Glen Markie 2

River Findhorn 3

Glen Markie 1

Note: your author was happy to walk this route – bikes are not much fun in deep heather!

to Tomatin 3km

R. Findhorn

Knockando

Dalmigavie Lo

Coignafearn/enterrich

Coignafearn Lodge

Dalbeg

bothy

Glen Markie

Sronlairig Lo public road/ends

600 650
550
500
450
400
350
300
250
200
150
100
50

0   5   10   15   20   25   30   35   40km

My wife and I have enjoyed the Monadhliath and Moray. From the wild mountains of the Corrieyairack to the beaches of Culbin Forest. Such contrast. I have, for once included a "way" - the Great Glen Cycle Route, though this is just as much a long distance walk. My reasons for including this, and not the West Highland Way (Book 3) are twofold. Firstly, the W.H.W is now well established (too well?) and the subject of several excellent guides before I came on the scene, and at the time of writing the G.G.C.R. is new. Secondly, and much more importantly the W.H.W. suffers from over-use and erosion, whilst the G.G.C.R. is such that it will withstand increased usage, being entirely on track, towpath and hard surfaced path - so no erosion problems...... The Monadhliath is one of our most sacred areas of wilderness - it is not peppered with Munros and therefore does not "suffer" the attention of great numbers of walkers. It is an area to be enjoyed equally a-wheel or on foot, with care.
I am concerned at the disappearance of some traceable paths from the O.S. maps - this will surely confirm the demise of these old 'roads'. I am also concerned at the lack of cycle access along parts of the old Fort Augustus railway, and the parallel General Wade road. These bits of our transport history should not be denied to the cyclist. We can only hope for a more enlightened attitude from landowners. In the meantime please comply with the signposting - voting with your feet (or wheels) only hardens attitudes!.... On that happy note(!) we are now off to The Angus Glens and the seventh book in this series, exploring Glen Doll, Glen Clova, and we may even meet the Old Man of Lochnagar! See you there.